WHEELING

DURING THE CIVIL WAR

Edited by Jeanne Finstein

Wheeling During the Civil War
Copyright © 2015
Copyright of each work belongs to its respective author.

Cover image: The crowded courtroom of the Wheeling Custom House is depicted in this illustration that appeared on the front cover of *Harper's Weekly* on July 6, 1861. The building is now called West Virginia Independence Hall. *(West Virginia and Regional History Center, WVU Libraries)*

ISBN-10: 0983371423
ISBN-13: 978-0-9833714-2-7

Contributors:

Margaret Brennan	David Javersak
John Bowman	Charles A. Julian
Robert DeFrancis	Bekah Karelis
Seán P. Duffy	Wilkes Kinney
Jeanne Finstein	Joseph Laker
Jon-Erik Gilot	Ed Phillips
Judi Hendrickson	Kate Quinn

For information or orders, contact:
Wheeling National Heritage Area Corporation
P.O. Box 350 • Wheeling, WV 26003
(304) 232-3087 • wheelingheritage.org

Printed in the USA by
Morris Publishing®
3212 E. Hwy. 30 • Kearney, NE 68847
800-650-7888 • www.morrispublishing.com

"We Have No Ordinary Task Before Us." As the Civil War raged on and West Virginia's statehood hung in the balance, these prophetic words were spoken by Arthur I. Boreman, the future first governor of the new state of West Virginia, at the Second Wheeling Convention in June of 1861. The Civil War years were eventful and often turbulent for the citizens of Wheeling and the rest of the western part of Virginia as they faced tasks that must have seemed insurmountable at the time. Yet their efforts bore fruit and are an inspiration to those who have benefited from them over the intervening years.

Although no battles were fought in or near Wheeling, its role in the birth of the new state of West Virginia was crucial. As a mainly industrial city, on the same northern latitude as Philadelphia, its many and varied products were marketed worldwide – using the Ohio River and Baltimore & Ohio Railroad as primary means of commerce. There was a slave market in town, but the number of local slaves was very low, and the economy of the area did not rely on them.

The war only added to long-standing rivalries between the eastern and western counties of Virginia. A large immigrant population in Wheeling felt a loyalty to the country as a whole, yet the established families often placed their loyalties with their home state of Virginia, causing more than one family to split – with brother fighting against brother and father against son.

To create this brief record of activities in Wheeling during that period, many members of the Wheeling Civil War Sesquicentennial Committee, along with other volunteers, conducted research and wrote the articles that follow. The compilation takes a month-by-month look at events in Wheeling during the Civil War years, using local newspapers as the main primary source and supplementing with a variety of other books and papers.

Every effort was made by all of the authors to avoid errors. We apologize for any mistakes that crept into the text.

No book such as this could be written without the help of many. In particular, the authors of the monthly summaries are to be thanked for their contributions; their names are listed with their articles. Most of their work appeared in the *Wheeling News-Register*, and we specifically thank Linda Comins for her ongoing editing skills and the editors of the newspaper for publishing the works during the four years of the sesquicentennial. Images for all of the articles are a worthwhile supplement. Thanks for help in finding those images go to Seán P. Duffy, Programming, Publicity, & Archives Coordinator, Ohio County Public Library; Erin Rothenbuehler, Co-Coordinator, Archives and Special Collections, Ohio County Public Library; Jon-Erik Gilot, Director of Archives & Records, Diocese of Wheeling-Charleston; Cheryl Harshman, West Liberty University Library; and historian Margaret Brennan. Wheeling's Civil War 150 logo was designed by Rhonda Baro. Thanks to Catherine Rakowski and John Cuthbert (West Virginia and Regional History Center, WVU Libraries) for locating and providing the image for use on the cover.

Funding for the layout and printing of the book was provided by the Wheeling National Heritage Area Corporation, Wheeling *Intelligencer*, and the *Wheeling News-Register*.

November and December 1860

By Margaret Brennan

Apart from the John Brown raid at Harper's Ferry on October 16-18, 1859, the path to civil war began with the election of Republican presidential candidate Abraham Lincoln on November 6, 1860.

The Wheeling newspaper, the *Daily Intelligencer*, under editors Archibald Campbell and John McDermot, was Republican leaning and showed that bias in its reporting. The Tuesday morning, November 6 paper highlighted the Virginia Republican ticket on the front page. There was a long, incisive editorial pointing out the inequality of the Virginia tax system as regards the eastern and western sections of the State, with slavery as the main obstacle. It noted that the Virginia Constitution states: "Taxation shall be equal and uniform throughout the commonwealth, and all property, other than slaves, shall be taxed in proportion to its value."

Obviously this set up an inequality in the sections' tax base, as the western portion of the state had fewer slaves. The paper quoted Henry Clay and Daniel Webster as being against the extension of slavery and urged people to support their sentiments and vote for Lincoln.

The *Intelligencer* also reported on various meetings throughout the city to support the candidates: Lincoln, John Bell of the Constitutional Union Party, John C. Breckenridge of the Southern Democratic Party, and Stephen A. Douglas of the Northern Democratic Party. Lincoln's supporters gathered at Washington Hall, and Breckenridge's men met at the Athenaeum. The Bell group made the biggest impression as "they marched through the streets with torches and bells of every description, the ringing of which and yelling for Bell could be heard in all directions." Mayor Andrew Wilson declared all taverns closed on voting day, and extra deputy sheriffs were appointed for each precinct.

On Wednesday, November 7, the paper reported the two Democrats with 1,292 votes had won the city, with Bell's tally at 936 and Lincoln's at 600. Individually Bell won the city and ultimately the state. The *Intelligencer* noted that, "Lincoln's vote in Ritchietown (present-day South Wheeling) was wonderful and was the talk on the streets and especially at the Court House all day." The editor reported that the vote was the largest ever tallied in the city, and the day went fairly well, although "at night men were intoxicated and traveled through the streets in a not very amiable manner." The Bell men were especially happy, yet the nation, led by the New England states, elected Abraham Lincoln. The paper noted it was the hottest and bitterest campaign since Andrew Jackson's time 30 years before.

Several interesting items were mentioned in the November 9 issue of the *Intelligencer*. Post-election rockets were set off in Center Wheeling. The LaBelle Mill boys fired their homemade cannon, "Old Garibaldi," 36 times, 33 for the states, one for Kansas, one for the Union, and one for Ritchietown. Ritchietown was praised profusely for the 164 votes for "Old Abe."

And Lincoln knew of the good Republican showing in Wheeling. A Springfield, Illinois, correspondent reported that when the 600 votes were announced in the State House with Lincoln present, he was immensely delighted. Yet people here were not that sure of Lincoln's first name, and the newspaper noted it was Abraham, not Abram.

With the 1860 election outcome, the gate to secession was opened. On November 8, it was reported that the South Carolina legislature had adopted a joint resolution "calling a convention of the people, the reorganization of the militia and preparations for the defense of the state." One writer surmised, "The secession of South Carolina seems inevitable." Georgia was also upset. The governor said his state was being unjustly targeted by certain northern laws and proposed taxing northern goods being brought in. At a mass meeting in Savannah on November 8, it was resolved that the election of Lincoln would not be accepted.

On November 12, the *Intelligencer* printed a scathing editorial attacking Virginia's tax laws and accusing eastern Virginia of governing the state for her own advantage, charging that western

Virginia did not even have proper representation in the state Senate. Looking ahead, one could see such views setting the stage for a push to separate from Virginia if she opted to turn against the Union.

The *Intelligencer* was filled with articles warning of the fallacy of forming a "Cotton Confederacy." "Instead of the ring of the woodman's axe, the merry carol of the boy at his plow, the hammer and saw of the artisan, will be heard the crack of the deadly rifle, the tread of armed men, the rattle of the drum and booming of the cannon, the wail of the widow and the cry of the orphan," surely prophetic words.

It seemed that immediately after the election, all eyes and editorials of the *Intelligencer* dealt with South Carolina as the state most resistant to the election. Indeed it was reported that, "for 20 years the spirit of disunion has been rife in South Carolina." And of course, the question emerged: "What will Virginia do?"

In the November 16 paper, a discussion of secession as a constitutional right was reprinted from the *New York Times*. Using 1788 letters from Alexander Hamilton and James Madison, the *Times* concluded that the question was settled before the Constitution was adopted. "It is treason to secede." One article from a Missouri newspaper cautioned the young men of the South to "keep cool; the government of the United States is a fixed fact, and one of these fine winter mornings you may wake up with a rather tight noose around your necks."

President James Buchanan, from Pennsylvania was caught in the middle of this controversy. His attorney general stated that no state had a constitutional right to secede. The President sent a message to Congress in early December. He declared that Congress could not coerce a state into submission when it attempted to withdraw from the Union. The *Daily Intelligencer* disagreed with the President's conclusion, and both the North and South dismissed Buchanan's views.

Governor John Letcher of Virginia appointed a commission of

ex-President John Tyler and two others to travel to South Carolina and urge her to delay her secessionist actions. Other states did the same but to no avail. The *Intelligencer* reported that, "the feeling against South Carolina is rapidly reaching the boiling point. Nobody but the very extremists sustain or justify her."

On December 14 there was a large Union meeting at the Wheeling Athenaeum as well as Union prayer meetings at the various churches. The people of the city understood what was at stake and generally denounced "the mad folly of secession." On December 21, the *Intelligencer* reported that on Thursday, December 20, the South Carolina convention had unanimously repealed the ordinance adopted May 23, 1788, ratifying the Constitution of the United States and all its amendments, and "that the union between South Carolina and other states, under the name of the United States of America, is hereby dissolved." The unthinkable had happened. Now the question, what next?

Abraham Lincoln appears to be pondering the future in this early portrait, taken in 1861. He could hardly have imagined what lay ahead. *(Library of Congress)*

December 1860 and January 1861
By Margaret Brennan

After the secession of South Carolina on December 20, 1860, there seemed to be a collective intake of breath, as the country tried to come to grips with what fast became an out-of-control chain of events. The first domino had fallen, and more would soon follow. South Carolina explained her actions in a declaration that saw "an increasing hostility on the part of the non-slave-holding States to the institution of slavery." The *Daily Intelligencer* printed a *New York Post* editorial that stated: "A few determined wicked men can make a great deal of trouble, as those perverse and obstinate South Carolina leaders prove." As the Senate pondered the situation, it also confirmed Edwin M. Stanton as Lincoln's attorney general.

Immediate attention was turned to the Fort Moultrie garrison in Charleston Harbor, as South Carolina immediately began to make threatening noises and set down demands. Adding to the tension was Mississippi, which indicated she would secede. All of this was happening at Christmas time. On December 25, there was a strong editorial stating, "There is no affinity between Eastern and Western Virginia. There never was. There is a very widespread sentiment in favor of a division of the State at the Blue Ridge."

On an ironic note, the December 27 Wheeling paper reported from Pittsburgh that there was a large order of heavy guns from the Allegheny Arsenal to be shipped south. The question was posed, "Shall Pennsylvania be disarmed and Charleston allowed to seize on Federal arms with which to overthrow the Union?" How this was resolved is unclear, but it was occurring in other places. A large handgun order was placed in Connecticut to be shipped south.

A strong editorial ran in the December 27 edition of the *Daily Intelligencer* warning the city of what could happen if Virginia became part of the Cotton Confederacy, given that Wheeling's trade routes went west and east rather than south. "We would be a one-horse cow pasture in about a year or less."

An interesting analysis of the Virginia slave trade appears in the December 28 paper. "The number of slaves in the State is about

475,000. The number annually exported [Virginia had more slaves than needed] is about 14,000, her most valuable product. At $500 per head, their value exceeds $7,000,000."

On December 28, the Wheeling paper reported, "A special dispatch this morning furnishes us the astounding news that the government troops have abandoned Fort Moultrie (on December 26) and taken up their quarters in Fort Sumter, further out in the harbor. The guns were spiked and the fort set on fire before being left."

In the midst of all these tensions, everyday life in Wheeling continued. On January 3, 1861, it was noted, "there was about six feet of water in the river yesterday." It was said that, "since the holidays, business has been universally dull in this city." Snow fell and brought out the sleighs and the boys on the sliding places. "We heard the merry jingling of sleigh bells."

On January 7, it was reported that, "the Union Men of Wheeling fired one hundred guns in honor of Major Anderson for the gallant stand he is taking in the defense of Fort Sumter."

On January 8, a lengthy statement from Waitman Willey of Morgantown was reprinted, in which he asks, "If secession commences, where will it end and when will it end. I shudder whenever I think of disunion."

On January 9, the *Intelligencer* noted that a company of cavalry from Carlisle Barracks, Pa., arrived by train to protect the arsenal at Harpers Ferry. On January 12, the second shoe fell, when it was reported from the Mississippi Convention that, "Mississippi by a nearly unanimous vote had seceded unconditionally from the Union." After that, it was off to the races. On January 10, Florida seceded, followed by Alabama on January 11, Georgia on January 19, Louisiana on January 26, and Texas on February 1. The seven secessionist states held a convention in Montgomery, Alabama, on February 4.

Again, the question, "what would Virginia do?" A bill to call a State Convention was passed on January 9, with the election of delegates to be held February 4. It was reported from Richmond that, "the very air here is charged with the electric thunder of war, in the street, at the Capitol, in the barroom, at the dinner table, nothing is heard but resistance to the general government." This did not bode well for the future.

As Governor of West Virginia from 1855 until 1860, Henry A. Wise became a strong advocate for Virginia's secession from the Union. One of his last official acts as Governor was to sign the death warrant of John Brown. After Virginia declared secession, Wise joined the Confederate army. Despite having no formal military training, he was commissioned as a brigadier general due to his political prominence and secessionist views. He left the state and settled in Richmond after the war. *(The History and Government of West Virginia by Richard Ellsworth Fast, 1901)*

February and March 1861
By Margaret Brennan

In the *Daily Intelligencer* for the months of February and March 1861, one saw a mixture of foreboding and hopefulness. The front page generally featured reports on the Virginia State Convention and articles on Washington. Page two highlighted local editorials, with more brief reports, and the third page ran stories of local interest, such as who was arrested and whose pigs ran loose.

February news began with the election of Wheeling delegates to the Virginia Convention. A Union working men's meeting at the Athenaeum numbered over 1,000 and nominated Chester Hubbard and Sherrard Clemens. The election on February 4 was "a glorious victory for the Union ticket," defeating Joseph Pendleton and Thomas Sweeney.

At this time, a Peace Convention was meeting in Washington, with 131 members from 21 states, although none of the seceded states attended. Headed by former President John Tyler, it was a desperate attempt to compromise and save the Union, but events would overtake this and other Congressional initiatives. Conference actions were duly reported in the Wheeling paper.

On February 13, it was noted that Major Anderson was able to buy supplies in Charleston for Fort Sumter, yet the South Carolina troops were preparing to attack the garrison. The Major was being pressured by his wife to resign his post, but he refused.

On February 14, the Wheeling newspaper editor boarded a crowded train for Steubenville to greet Abraham Lincoln. At 2:30 p.m., a gaily decorated train, with flags flying, brought the President-elect into town. There was a lengthy description of the events and Lincoln's short speech. The editor thought he looked fatigued.

Jefferson Davis was inaugurated President of the seven Confederate States of America at Montgomery, Alabama on Monday, February 18, and the newspaper printed his address. It was interesting to note that Davis and Lincoln left for their respective capital cities on the same day, but the Confederacy wanted to beat the Union to the punch, which it did. At the time, the Confederate states consisted of, in order of secession, South Carolina, Mississippi, Florida, Alabama, Georgia, Louisiana, and Texas, to be followed later by Virginia, Arkansas, Tennessee, and North Carolina.

A special reporter was sent to the Richmond Convention, and all the speeches were duly covered as secession was debated. Former Governor Henry A. Wise of Virginia said if Virginia didn't secede, he would leave the state. Meanwhile, it was reported that there was dissension in the ranks of the new Confederate government at Montgomery, and the big troublemaker seemed to be South Carolina!

The February 27 paper noted that Wheeling was well represented at the Virginia Convention as various citizens had gone to observe the proceedings. Meanwhile, Mr. Lincoln visited the Congress and caused quite a stir. He had entered Washington under cover of secrecy and in disguise after a death threat had prompted Mrs. Lincoln and his advisors to insist that he change his plans, much to his distaste.

On March 4, the newspaper ran a strong editorial on how "the South is deceived by the idea that its great staple, cotton, rules the trade of the world. They are not as independent as they are apt to fancy." On Tuesday, March 5, the front page featured the previous day's inauguration of President Lincoln and ran his address. "Mr. Lincoln was much cheered."

On March 14, a speech by Waitman T. Willey at the convention pointed out that the state had a hefty debt, and if war came the people could not endure the taxes. The paper complained that the convention was costing $2,000 a day, had already run up an $80,000 bill, and the delegates should just pack up and go home as nothing significant was being accomplished.

On more mundane matters, the citizens of Wheeling were urged to plant more shade trees and grape vines, hogs were running loose and a German and an Irishman went to court over one, and the young boys loved their games of marbles. Spring lifted the peoples' spirits, but Easter joy would prove short lived. War was just around the corner.

Morgantown native Waitman Willey was an early activist for West Virginia's statehood. He later served as a United States Senator (1863-1871), representing the newly formed state. *(West Virginia Independence Hall Foundation)*

April 1861

By Jeanne Finstein

Excitement filled the air in the entire country in April of 1861. South Carolina had seceded from the Union in December, followed quickly by six other states. In February, the South created a government with its own constitution and president – Jefferson Davis – and seized federal forts within its boundaries. President Abraham Lincoln, who had been inaugurated on March 4, refused to accept the states' secession and hoped to resolve the issues without war. But on April 12 Fort Sumter was fired upon and surrendered to the Confederacy – marking the war's beginning.

Wheeling was caught up in this excitement, as citizens in the entire state of Virginia faced the question of whether to join their southern counterparts in secession or remain loyal to the Union. An intense rivalry was already in place in the state between the capital Richmond with its southern traditions and the industrialized Wheeling – the largest city in the western part of the state and heavily tied through business interests to the North. Although many of the old-line families of Wheeling pledged loyalty to Richmond, the prevailing spirit of most citizens of Wheeling was in support of the Union.

The pro-Union *Daily Intelligencer*, under editor Archibald W. Campbell, kept its readers informed of the national events. A front-page reprint of an article from the *New York World* on April 1 questioned the future of slavery and opened with the statement, "It is probable that before the year 2000 of the Christian era, human slavery will have become extinct." But the article continued with the ominous statement, "We do not suppose that slavery will be ever extinguished on this continent by the mere force of public opinion."

Slavery had never been much of an issue in the western part of Virginia. The 1860 census reported the total population of the state as nearly 1.5 million, nearly one-third of whom were slaves. However, the counties to the west of the Alleghenies – one third of the total number of counties– reported only 5000 slaves – one-hundredth of the total number of slaves. There were only about 100 slaves in Ohio County at the time, many of whom were house servants.

The local paper also ran stories and advertisements typical of the time period. Parents were reminded to have their children vaccinated against smallpox; citizens were urged to plant trees; and annual subscriptions to the Wheeling library were reduced from five to three dollars. Ads featured "Ayer's Sarsparilla for purifying the blood" and "Udolpho Wolfe's Aromatic Schnapps: a superlative tonic, diuretic, anti dyspeptic, and invigorating cordial – pure Holland gin for medicinal and private use." But there was also an ad for "Col. Sam Holt's revolving fire arms," and dry goods merchant John Roemers offered a large lot of prints, muslins, and checks "in view of the preservation of the Union."

The state's watershed moment occurred on April 17, 1861, when the Virginia Convention voted for secession and announced that a vote of ratification by the people would be held on May 23. Ohio County's representatives to the Convention, Chester D. Hubbard and Sherrard Clemens, strongly favored the Union and fled Richmond immediately, perhaps in fear for their lives but certainly eager to report to their constituents and promote the Union cause back home.

When he arrived back in Wheeling, Hubbard began strongly agitating for the organization of military companies for home defense. Patriotic fervor was particularly strong in the blue-collar neighborhoods of East, Centre and South Wheeling. A meeting was held in Wheeling's Fourth Ward (East Wheeling) on April 18, and the Rough and Ready Guards were formed, with 40 men enrolled. The first on the list was James W. Bodley, listed in the 1860 census as a 44-year-old bricklayer with a wife and six children. The Iron Guards, made up primarily of men from the LaBelle nail works in South Wheeling, followed soon after.

Meanwhile, President Lincoln issued a call for 75,000 men to "suppress" the Confederate states and "cause the laws to be duly executed." The Rough and Ready Guards and Iron Guards became a part of that number as Companies A and B of the First (West) Virginia Infantry. Their term of service was three months – at the time, thought to be a long enough period to settle the conflict. Ultimately, over 2.5 million men served the Union cause, and another estimated million fought for the Confederacy. And the war lasted four years, rather than three months, resulting in the deaths of more than 600,000 men.

On April 19 a rumor circulated that Virginia Governor John Letcher had issued an order to one or more of the state militia companies to take and occupy the Custom House in Wheeling – now known as West Virginia Independence Hall. The rumor spread like wildfire, and within an hour, hundreds of people reportedly congregated at the Custom House to "tender their services for its defense, and the utmost excitement prevailed." Mayor Andrew J. Sweeney and other city authorities promised to take all necessary precautions for the defense of the building, and the crowd quietly dispersed. That same evening, Sweeney swore in 100 extra policemen to ensure order in the city and published a request to citizens to "refrain from violent and harsh expressions."

The *Wheeling Union*, a paper that despite its name had decided Southern sympathies, criticized Lincoln for declaring war on the Confederacy. An editorial in the *Intelligencer* took the opposite view. "The President has not declared war against the South, but Jefferson Davis and Company have declared war by their acts against the United States." The *Intelligencer* also kept track of enlistment activities and reported on April 25 that there were three companies in Ritchietown (South Wheeling), three in the 5th Ward (Centre Wheeling), one in the 4th Ward (East Wheeling), and one in the 3rd Ward (between what are now named 11th and 14th Streets). The company size of each ranged from 80 to 100 men. A company from North Wheeling was formed soon afterwards.

By the end of the month, the paper published a call for a

convention to be held in Wheeling on May 13, and all citizens – no matter which side they supported – awaited that date with great anticipation.

Chester D. Hubbard was one of the Ohio County delegates to the Virginia Convention that debated Virginia's secession from the Union. Both he and his fellow delegate, Sherrard Clemens, opposed secession and found themselves in a distinct minority. *(Library of Congress)*

By Kate Quinn

When on April 17, 1861, the Virginia Convention at Richmond voted to leave the Union, they set off a wave of patriotism in Wheeling never before seen in this city. The supervisor of the Virginia Mill in Benwood was hung in effigy for his sympathy with the Southern cause; the city's merchants resolved to pay no taxes to the state of Virginia; Major Oakes of the U.S. Army arrived in Wheeling to inspect several companies of would-be soldiers; and work began at the fairgrounds on Wheeling Island to construct a military training and staging camp.

Meanwhile, Union troops transported by train through Baltimore caused a riot in that city where residents had not yet decided where their loyalties lay. Here in the western part of Virginia a meeting was held at Clarksburg to decide what to do about the secession vote. Francis Pierpont spoke for two and one half hours and reminded those in attendance that all lawyers, magistrates, and judges had taken an oath to uphold the Constitution of the United States. He asked Waitman T. Willey what his intentions were for the future, and Willey replied that he intended to die under the Stars and Stripes and would never live in a Southern Confederacy that is carried on under a flag that has no better motto than a rattlesnake!

On May 10, the first company of Virginia (Federal) Infantry, Company A (3 months service), under Captain A. H. Britt, was mustered into federal service in Wheeling. A pro-Union demonstration was held, and the paper reported, "On Saturday night, it having been generally known that Mr. [John S.] Carlile and other distinguished gentlemen were in the city and at the McLure House, an immense concourse of people collected in the street in front of the hotel for the purpose of calling out some speeches. About 9 o'clock the Iron Guards marched up in front of the McLure with flying colors and martial music amid the cheers and shouts of the assembled crowd which at this time could not have numbered less than 1500 or 2000 people. The German band was out and played the Star Spangled Banner, Hail Columbia, and other patriotic airs in very fine style. No sooner had the military paraded in front of the house than the cry went up for 'Carlile! Carlile!' from all quarters and with deafening unanimity."

Carlile eventually came out on a balcony and said that he was "very unwell" but then went on to give a rousing patriotic speech ending in, "I have always believed that if the Union men in the border slave states would take a firm, decided and bold position, they could put down secession in their midst, and could and would be instrumental in restoring peace and harmony to the whole country." Mr. Pierpont's speech was much more humorous.

Newspaper ads for the "Golden Bee Hive Store" (Stone and Thomas) touted that they carried miles of red, white, and blue bunting. Other ads were for American flags, drums and fifes, hoop skirts, shaker hoods, cane hoops, Mason City salt, Durham cattle, and Cotswold sheep. L.J. & I Phillips published a letter they had sent to a mercantile house in New York City asking them to supply blue fatigue caps and saying, "We expect to clean out the traitors in a very short time after we begin. I hope you will be as liberal as possible as they are for our Western Virginia army to fight for the Star Spangled Banner."

It was reported that 700 barrels of flour left Cincinnati on the steamer *Reliance* consigned to Pittsburgh, but were instead delivered to secessionists in Wheeling, who put them on the B & O to rebel troops. There were numerous reports of inebriated troops on the streets of Wheeling, but no reports of arrest as these troops were on their way to Maryland to fight for the Union. The paper also carried instructions for making a flag and reported that patriotic contributions from Northern States totaled $23 million! Locally a plea was sent out for contributions to purchase or make uniforms for local soldiers.

Pay for soldiers was reported as follows: Colonel - $218 per month, Captain - $118, Corporal - $22, and private - $20. All received part of their pay in rations, and privates were to get 160 acres of land.

In a ceremony at the Custom House on May 13 the Union flag was raised, and the new collector of customs, Thomas Hornbrook, Esq. received his appointment. Five thousand people attended, and the paper stated, "Never was there any such a time in this loyal, little city before." The next day the Wheeling Convention began at Washington Hall. Seventeen counties of Virginia sent 536 delegates. Committees were delegated to decide on Credentials and State and Federal Regulations. The Constitution clearly stated that a new state could only be formed with the permission of the existing state (Virginia). It was decided to wait until the May 23 referendum to see how the people of western Virginia felt on the issue of a new state.

Southern sympathizers organized their own companies of soldiers. Daniel Shriver recruited a company of men to be known as the Shriver Grays. They were later mustered into service as Company G of the 27th Virginia Infantry. Their gray uniforms were secretly made purportedly to be worn at a local wedding, and they drilled in the local cornfields at night.

Camp Carlile on Wheeling Island was now occupied, and the men were well supplied with straw for bedding, quilts, blankets and food. One soldier said he "never had such a relish." They drilled for 3 hours a day. When Francis Pierpont was recognized in the camp, the "boys" insisted on a speech, and he obliged. The call for more Bibles and blankets for the camp rang out. For just 25 cents one could take an omnibus to the island to watch the dress parade. On May 23 Col. Benjamin Franklin Kelley was unanimously elected commander of the camp, and then the soldiers were given leave to go home to vote.

The day before, the first Union casualty of the War took place when Confederates in Grafton killed Bailey Brown, a private. Headlines in the next day's paper stated that "War Begins" as troops marched into Fairfax, Virginia, and Union troops arrived at Grafton. Reports from that city to the *Intelligencer* stated that 500 cavalry were on their way to attack Wheeling. The rumors proved false.

On May 25, secessionists burned railroad trestles at Farmington and Mannington, and General George McClellan ordered the troops at Camp Carlile to move to Grafton to protect the railroad. The men were mustered, and orders from Col. Kelley were read at midnight to soldiers standing in a drenching rain. All night long thunder and lightning pounded the city and delayed the departure until daylight when the men marched through the city to the B & O depot. Greeted by crowds of women waving handkerchiefs and weeping, the train departed at 7 a.m. On that same day a rhino, kangaroos, goats, monkeys, and ponies paraded the streets of Wheeling encouraging citizens to visit Dan Rice's "Great Show" at the corner of 5th and John Street featuring the March of Lanterns and Ella Zoyara, Queen of the Ring with her dancing steed.

On May 30th, the newspaper published General McClellan's proclamation telling the people of Western Virginia that he had ordered troops from Ohio to cross into Western Virginia to protect those who supported the constitution of the United States. By this date these troops had reached Grafton, and the stage was set for the first land battle of the Civil War.

The U.S. Army organized Camp Carlile on Wheeling Island as a military training and staging camp. Because of its location near the Suspension Bridge, the camp was readily available to Wheeling, and it quickly became crowded, not only with incoming troops but with curious citizens as well. This photo was taken in 1862. *(Herb Bierkortte Collection)*

June 1861

By Margaret Brennan

June 1861 was a pivotal month for western Virginia. We know that Virginia had passed an ordinance of secession on April 17, and on April 22 large protest meetings in Clarksburg and Morgantown were held. On May 13, the First Wheeling Convention assembled its 436 delegates, deciding to suspend action until the May 23 vote of the people. Of course, the eastern Virginia populous ratified secession, but the western counties did not. A Second Wheeling Convention was called for June 11.

Much was happening in Wheeling before then. On June 1, the *Intelligencer* noted that so many fire companies had enlisted in the army, the people were urged to be extra cautious. Hundreds of Ohio and Indiana troops were crossing the river from Bellaire to Benwood to take the trains to the Grafton area, "all large, hardy, handsome men jolly and jovial, and extremely anxious to find some secessionists." Thirty secessionists from Wheeling, including Philip Henry Moore, editor of the *Wheeling Union*, left town by boat, in fear of their lives.

The June 4 newspaper reported the June 3 success at the Battle of Philippi and the fact that Col. Benjamin Kelley was not mortally wounded, as first thought. Kelley's friends in Wheeling insisted that Dr. John Frissell be sent by train to assist the regimental surgeon, Col. Joseph Thoburn, in his care. The prisoners charged in the burning of the B & O bridges were being housed in pens at Camp Carlile.

Upcoming newspapers gave more detail on the Philippi battle. The First Virginia (Union) Regiment from Wheeling was the lead infantry, but there was ongoing criticism of their poor equipment. A large secessionist flag captured in the battle was brought to Wheeling and presented to the ladies of LaBelle nail works. And the city was astonished that Major Alonzo Loring, the sheriff of Ohio County, had been arrested here and was being taken to Grafton on a charge of treason. He was later released.

The June 8 *Intelligencer* gave the outcome of the voting for convention delegates. Daniel Lamb, James Paxton, George Harrison, and Chester Hubbard would represent local interests.

The first meeting of the Second Wheeling Convention with about 100 delegates from 34 counties convened at Washington Hall Tuesday, June 11 at 2:00 p.m. and remained in session two weeks. Rev. Gordon Battelle opened with a prayer. Various committees were appointed, and the delegates agreed to meet at 10:00 a.m. June 12. At that time, Arthur T. Boreman of Parkersburg was elected president, Gibson L. Cranmer of Wheeling secretary, and Thomas Hornbrook of Wheeling sergeant at arms. Boreman gave a short speech, stating, "We have no ordinary task before us. We have come here to institute a government for ourselves. It requires stout hearts, men of courage, of unfaltering determination." A working committee of 13 was appointed to prepare and report the business of the convention. It was decided that the next meeting would be held in the U.S. Court Room at the Custom House.

On June 13, 1861, John Carlile of Clarksburg read to the assembly a Declaration of the People of Virginia. Much like the Declaration of Independence, it listed the grievances against the Richmond government and concluded that all its recent actions were void and all its offices vacated. James Paxton of Wheeling then gave an impassioned speech. Francis Pierpont of Fairmont threw his weight behind the resolution, and it was adopted by a vote of 56-0, the same number that signed the original Declaration.

The next day, June 14, Carlile reported an Ordinance for the Re-organization of the State Government, declaring that the convention at Wheeling represented all the people of Virginia and that new state officers would be elected by the convention and be required to take an oath upholding the Constitution of the United States. The ordinance would be considered June 15 at 11:00 a.m.

For the next several days, delegates debated the ordinance reorganizing the government of Virginia, and it was unanimously adopted on June 19, after a stirring speech by Francis Pierpont. All understood that it was a necessary first step to what most saw was the inevitable separation from eastern Virginia.

On Thursday, June 20, the first order of business was the signing of the specially prepared parchment copy of the Declaration of Rights. Eighty-three gentlemen signed the paper. Then came the election of state officers. Daniel Lamb presented the name of Francis Pierpont for Governor, who was unanimously elected, offered a few remarks and was sworn in. In short order, Daniel Polsley of Mason County was elected Lieutenant Governor, and the five-member council to the Governor, including Daniel Lamb and James Paxton of Wheeling, were sworn in. The Attorney General, elected later, would be James Wheat of Ohio County.

The people of Wheeling showed their approval of the proceedings by ringing bells, banging drums, and setting off cannons. The newly elected officials visited Camp Carlile, where they witnessed a dress parade of 600 soldiers, followed by the firing of salutes. Thankfully this would be the closest Wheeling would get to the sounds of battle. Other parts of western Virginia would not be so lucky.

As leader of the First [West] Virginia Infantry, Col. Benjamin Franklin Kelley led the Union troops at the Battle of Philippi, considered the first land battle of the Civil War. Although severely wounded in that skirmish, he returned to service and later achieved the ranks of Brigadier General and Brevet Major General. He survived the war and is buried in Arlington National Cemetery. *(Library of Congress)*

July 1861
By Bekah Karelis

As the summer months of 1861 progressed, tensions mounted in the field and began erupting. Early in the month, skirmishes erupted across western Virginia in such places as Harper's Ferry, Glenville, and Laurel Hill.

Early on a Sunday, July 2, an ugly-looking effigy of Jefferson Davis was discovered suspended on the flagpole at the First Ward Hose House in Wheeling. It hung on the pole all day Sunday and attracted a great deal of attention. It was labeled "Jeff Davis – a warning to traitors."

An advertisement appeared in the newspaper that Captain Craig of the Quartermaster's Office was interested in purchasing 100 draft war horses. The inspection of horses would happen at Camp Carlile on the Island. Very early on inspection day, hundreds of horses were reported "trotting and whinnying" across both bridges to the Island. "Some of the horses looked as though they had been turned out to die and only resurrected for this occasion. Others were tolerable specimens of the equine species, and some were really good. Good horses were purchased for the average amount of 100 dollars." The purchased horses were driven from town to Benwood where they were shipped to Grafton.

Wheeling received a number of arms donated to the city by the state of Massachusetts. Two thousand arms were stored at the Custom House where they awaited the decision of the new Governor of Virginia as how best to use them.

Meanwhile, troops were passing through the city of Wheeling on their way to other cities to the East. A cavalry company from Illinois en-route to Grafton came through Wheeling. They crossed the bridge four abreast and marched down Market Street. At their head was a Wheeling German Brass Band. They were drawn up in front of the Custom House, where they were addressed by Governor Pierpont.

"The custom house in Wheeling is now the grand center of attraction. It is not only a Custom House, a State house, and a Post

Office but also an arsenal. Some 75 boxes of arms, in addition to those already there, were deposited yesterday. These will make a formidable armament when properly distributed, as they soon will be."

Some time before, the Virginia Convention ordered the halt of work on the Weston Lunatic Asylum in order to save the $27,000 deposited in the local bank to fund the project. Captain List was commissioned by Pierpont to take the money before "Letcher's government" would appropriate it elsewhere. The expedition left Clarksburg on Saturday evening and arrived in Weston at 5 a.m. Sunday. They had at their forefront a band playing the Star Spangled Banner, to announce their early morning arrival. Captain List demanded the money in the name of the State of Virginia, and it was handed over to him with no resistance. A six-man guard accompanied the money back to Wheeling where it was deposited in the Northwestern Bank "and will be used by those to whom it truly belongs – the true State government."

The newspaper reported, "The loyal Government through General McClellan and Capt. List put a stop to that arrangement by going down there and taking the money. We think this end of the State has made a pretty good thing out of it. We need money almost as badly as they do down at Richmond, and are in no particular need of a lunatic asylum. They can have all the Lunatic Asylum they want, if they will give us the money. Just now coin is infinitely preferable to crazy people."

The battle of Corrick's Ford in Tucker County on July 13 saw the war's first casualty of a general. General George McClellan officially announced the death of Confederate General Robert S. Garnett in a dispatch, "You will, ere this, no doubt, be informed of the unhappy fate of General Garnett, who fell while acting the part of a gallant soldier." On July 17, General Garnett's remains arrived in Wheeling en-route to his home in Virginia. A metal coffin was sent from Wheeling to Grafton to retrieve the body. "The depot was literally packed with people upon the arrival of the train, all being anxious to get a peep at the coffin."

Union forces defeated the Confederates at the Battle of Rich Mountain on July 11. The newspaper reported, "A battle was fought yesterday afternoon at Rich Mountain, where the enemy, numbering about two thousand, under command of Col. [John] Pegram were strongly entrenched. A desperate fight immediately ensued, which lasted about an hour and a half, resulting in the loss of 60 of the enemy killed, a large number wounded and prisoners – some of the latter are officers. The rebels retreated precipitously, leaving behind 6 cannons, a large number of horses, wagons, and camp equipage and the loss on our side is about 20 killed and 40 wounded."

By the middle of July, the majority of Confederate forces were driven from the areas of modern-day West Virginia. It was this success, combined with confidence in General McClellan's skills, that gave political leaders in Wheeling the impetus to continue with their plans of separating from eastern Virginia. The campaigns led in western Virginia earned McClellan a promotion and enormous popularity here in Wheeling. In fact, he was received in Wheeling on July 25, 1861, while returning to Washington after the Union's defeat at the battle of Bull Run. The newspaper reported, "Gen. McClellan was serenaded in front of the McLure House, and hundreds of people collected to see him."

Closer to home, Bethany had begun to organize a Home Guard that already numbered 45 (50 being the required quota to entitle them to arms). A Captain Boring, "the head devil in secession mischief," was arrested and released on parole of honor. Centre Wheeling formed a company called "Pierpont Guards" in honor of the Governor; the company numbered sixty members and was provided with muskets, uniforms, and equipment for service.

A letter appeared in the newspaper from prisoners on Wheeling Island. Life as a prisoner at Camp Carlile did not sound too pleasant from the way it's described. "We the prisoners of Capt. Planke's Co.,

2nd Regiment, VA militia, now on the Island, in the guardhouse, would most respectfully ask you, to publish the following in your paper: We have been here now for 3 weeks, sleeping on the bare ground, with neither straw below, nor cover above us, without clean shirts, not a chance to clean ourselves, consequently vermin will appear, and did so. Our rations are so short, that we hardly can keep from starving, and not even for money can we get any nourishment. We have often asked to enter complaint before the higher offices, but they never respected us; we ask no more, than to be treated like human beings and not worse than animals."

This well-known illustration was published by *Harper's Weekly* on July 6, 1861. It depicts delegates to the Second Wheeling Convention as they met in the courtroom of the Custom House and considered the possibility of forming a new state. The building is now called West Virginia Independence Hall. (*Harper's Weekly*)

August 1861
By Robert DeFrancis

The pages of Wheeling's *Daily Intelligencer* in August 1861, printed under the hand of famed editor Archibald W. Campbell, were full of details of life in the city that now was now home to the Restored Government of Virginia, soldiers training at Camp Carlile on the Island, and constant talk of "treason and secession."

Campbell's *Intelligencer*, which he bought in 1856 at the age of 23, along with John McDermot, almost immediately aligned itself with the emerging Republican Party. Initially, this choice was unpopular among Wheeling's elite business interests, and it was thought the newspaper would fold quickly. Of course, such was not to be, and Campbell's allegiance to the party of Abraham Lincoln, by 1861, enabled him to boast in his smaller masthead that the *Daily Intelligencer* had the "Largest Circulation of any Paper in Western Virginia." By April 1861, the young yet seasoned and respected editor was in the midst of a campaign of words supporting the "patriotic men in North-Western Virginia" and in staunch opposition to Eastern Virginia's interests and the Confederacy.

On Tuesday, August 6, after exclaiming the "good news" that the Government had promised new shipments to Wheeling of "arms and equipments," Campbell's newspaper said, "We shall soon be in the position to wipe out the last vestiges of treason and secession from our borders. The invaders are already driven ignominiously beyond our limits, and our gallant troops are pursuing them. Let us make the work complete. Let us show the Eastern tyrants that we are a free people, that we always intend to remain free and that the haughty yoke of Eastern Virginia has been lifted from our necks forever."

Surely those of us now discussing issues surrounding the U.S. Constitution would have been equally taken by an argument advanced that August by Campbell. In arguing that the conflict is "not a war against slavery," the editor said ... "it is a war for the integrity of the Government, for the Constitution, and the supremacy of laws." Later in the same columns, he wrote, "We must succeed. This government must not, cannot fail. The Constitution – which is based upon principles immutable, and upon which rest the rights of man, and the hopes and expectations of those who love freedom throughout the civilized world – must be maintained."

The *Daily Intelligencer* as well was reporting that August in detail and in depth on the Second Wheeling Convention. On August 14, several columns of type reporting convention actions were introduced with the following statement, "It appears to be pretty generally understood now that the Convention is going to take some steps toward dividing this State. Just what it is to be cannot yet be determined."

A week later, on August 21, under a small headline reading "The New State Ordinance," the newspaper said, "We would call attention this morning to the report of the proceedings of the Convention yesterday, by which it will be seen that the body has at last agreed upon a harmonious conclusion in favor of a division of the State." Campbell's paper thereafter printed the ordinance as reported from the committee but promised to print the full ordinance, with amendments incorporated, the next day "so that our readers can have it to file away for reference."

Campbell said, "The measure is not quite all that the more ardent divisionists would have preferred, but if we are not greatly mistaken in the temper of the people, and in what will be the expression of it in the election to be held, we shall all be citizens of the State of Kanawha before many months roll round."

As news spread of the state's potential division, Campbell a few days later reprinted a piece from the *Morgantown Star*, which opined, "The name of the proposed new State formed from this portion of Virginia – Kanawha – is not the one we would have given, but it is, nevertheless, a very pretty one, but not so good as 'New Virginia,' or 'West Virginia.' We still love the name of Virginia, and now that our Convention has commenced breaking the chains forged for us by the tyrants of the East, we are proud to say that we were born in West Virginia."

Apparently, it was common for newspapers a century and a half ago to report about each other. In August alone, the *Daily Intelligencer* discussed at length the loathsome behavior of a newspaper in St. Clairsville with alleged Confederate leanings. A letter from the editor of the *Knoxville Whig*, W.G. Brownlow, pointed out that he as a principled man "will yield to the demand of an armed mob" by turning over "to them our office and what little property we have" but "we shall refuse, most obstinately refuse, to the day of our death to think or speak favorably of such a Confederacy as this... ." And, Campbell put in a short plug for *The Wellsburg Herald*, which, he said, was "being published at a loss to the editor." Along with its "invaluable services to the Union cause, it is a local auxiliary to the best interests of" Brooke and Hancock counties, and "we hope that our people generally in Western Virginia who are able to do so will lend the *Herald* a helping hand."

The newspaper took great interest also in the goings on at Camp Carlile. Several editions reported on the soldiers as well as the prisoners at the Wheeling Island camp. One short story reported, "A soldier who had been guilty of some misdemeanor, yesterday ran across the suspension bridge pursued by two officers. He was captured at the West end of the bridge with the loss of his entire coat tail. He was taken to jail." Reporting on prisoners at the camp, the paper indicated that they were being treated well. "One of the prisoners jocosely remarked that in their little circle there was the utmost toleration of opinion and greatest liberality of feeling – that the guard house was the only place in Virginia, East or West, where a man was allowed to express his sentiments."

Under the phrase "A Good Joke," the newspaper reported, "Ever since the establishment of Camp Carlile and since the first secessionist was ejected from the grounds, it has been regarded as a capital joke among Union men to have their friends put out by a squad of soldiers. The soldiers are not expected to know everybody and whenever a commissioned officer is advised that there is a secessionist on the grounds he forthwith issues an order to have him ejected. The person so ejected may be a Union man or not – the soldiers do not know and frequently waggish fellows have their friends ejected just for the fun of the thing. It is by no means an uncommon thing to see a Union man going out of the camp at the point of the bayonet, looking very silly, while his friends are bursting their sides with laughter. A case of this kind occurred yesterday to the infinite amusement of everybody who witnessed it."

Eugene Zane, ostensibly a member of the extended Zane family, would not have been amused by the *Intelligencer*'s report of "Arrest of Secessionists." In fact, it is easy to imagine that the newspaper was tossed across the room by more than one Zane who read it that day, August 31, 1861.

"Last evening six secessionists were arrested ... at the house of Dr. Alfred Hughes, corner of Fourth and Quincy streets. It seems that on Thursday evening, a batch of young men succeeded in leaving the city for the rebel army, and it was suspected that the six persons found at Hughes' designed doing the same thing.

"Three of the young men were citizens: Jacob Swietzer, John Goshorn and Eugene Zane," and the other three were prisoners who had been released from captivity, one who had been in the hospital for an extended time and two who were at Camp Carlile. The men "were taken to the Custom House, where a large crowd soon collected." With no additional details, the newspaper then reported that Goshorn was released and that Swietzer and the ex-prisoners were "sent over to Camp Carlile." As to Zane, the *Intelligencer* reported, "Zane was released, as it was thought he was not likely to go to the rebel army or anywhere else, except in the house when it rains."

Dr. Hughes' house was searched but nothing of a "contraband character" was found. Hughes ultimately was arrested for disloyalty in 1861, tried in April of 1862, and spent eight months in Camp Chase in Columbus after being sent there in June of that year.

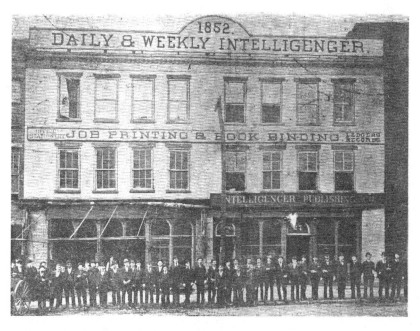

During the Civil War, the offices of the Wheeling *Daily Intelligencer* probably looked very much like this later image. Owned by staunch Unionist Archibald Campbell, the newspaper strongly supported West Virginia statehood. *(Ohio County Public Library)*

By Kate Quinn

Life went on in Wheeling during September of 1861 despite the war. Although it brought excitement to the town, the war barely caused a ripple in the day-to-day life of our city that month.

At the beginning of the month Camp Carlile had only 300 men stationed on its ragged turf, though Confederate prisoners were often stockaded there. Two prisoners from Parkersburg ("neither of them had clothes enough on their persons to wad a gun") were among those imprisoned at the site. The prisoners wrote to the newspaper complaining about conditions at the Camp, but a reporter who investigated was stuck in the rear with a bayonet by guards and let it be known that the men seemed happy enough. They were playing horseshoes when he visited. By the third week in September, Camp Carlile had been completely renovated with new tents. Nine hundred men were now accommodated there, and Col. Anasanell of the 1st Virginia Cavalry was in charge.

The Pierpont Guards went scouting in Triadelphia and after searching several houses brought back a number of rifles, which they took from secessionists.

Fashions for fall called for capes with no trimming since such luxury had suddenly become too expensive.

It was decided that the State Constitutional convention would be held in Wheeling on November 15, and 39 counties would be represented. If the people adopted the constitution, and the Legislature granted its consent, then the state could apply for admission to the Union. There were many letters to the editor complaining about the proposed name of "Kanawha." Many stated that it was too hard to spell, too hard to pronounce (even today people from that area can only manage to get out two of the syllables), and was a concession to politicians from that area. Wheeling folks were "true Virginians" and wanted the world to know it. They felt the name West Virginia conveyed that patriotism.

The Emperor of Russia sent a letter to President Lincoln wishing success with the war. This powerful ally promised that the

Russians would not allow any European countries to interfere in our government.

The existence of "Wheeling dollars" was denied by the *Intelligencer* until a week later when a soldier wrote to the paper saying he had been paid by the Quartermaster in Wheeling dollars and ads for local stores began to proclaim that they would accept the paper currency. These bills were issued by a U.S. mint and showed the charter number of the banks authorized to issue them, which included the First National Bank of Wheeling and the Merchants and Mechanics Bank. The Custom House was said to be holding between one quarter and one half million dollars in gold to be used to pay the soldiers.

Still more volunteers were needed, and the newspaper ran the following announcement, "Attention volunteers!!! Your citizens are in peril. Let every man that has the arm and nerve for a soldier fly to the rescue. Neither laggards nor cowards are wanted." Joseph Thoburn by order of General Benjamin Kelley, signed the notice. The call was answered by Ann Watson who tried to enlist, but was instead arrested for "parading in men's clothes."

Among the notable citizens of the Wheeling area who did sign up were Dr. Robert Hazlett, who served as a surgeon for the duration of the war; August Rolf, a successful businessman who served on the Board of County Commissioners; Henry Hornbrook, whose father was an aide de camp to governors Pierpont and Boreman and whose uncle owned the land that is now Wheeling Park; William and John Arthur, two Wheeling brothers who held various positions in the city; the Curtis family of West Liberty, who distinguished themselves in battle; Milton Worls, ancestor of Randy Worls of Oglebay Foundation; and Felix Crago, a teacher and later president of West Liberty College (now University).

Dr. John Frissell performed surgery on General Kelly and successfully removed the ball that had been lodged in his shoulder since the "affair" at Philippi. It was reported to be quite painful, but healing well.

A donation of $800 ($20,400 in today's money) was sent to Mayor Andrew J. Sweeney from the citizens of San Francisco to be used to support the widows and orphans of the First Virginia Regiment.

As is usual in the fall, county fairs were held at Washington, Pennsylvania, and Belmont County, Ohio, although it was reported that the Ohio fair "didn't amount to much." On a more serious side, September 26 was set aside by President Lincoln as a day of fasting and prayer. All stores were closed, churches were open, and the people of Wheeling solemnly observed the day.

At the beginning of the month the river had been at four feet ten inches, but after very heavy downfalls it rose to 37 feet putting most of the island, including Camp Carlile, under water. This was one of the many "Great Pumpkin Floods," which were so named due to the large number of pumpkins torn from the vines in the farmers' fields and filling the river. One of the guy wires of the Suspension Bridge was swept away and "enough driftwood was passed down to keep the Southern Confederates in fuel for six months." The flood destroyed all cornfields in the valley of Wheeling Creek "for three or four miles west of Bridgeport," and great numbers of barns, outhouses and logs filled the river from shore to shore.

Life went on in our "little" city of 14,000 people as the war raged elsewhere, but the gravity of the times was still obvious. In his Message to Congress, President Lincoln stated, "And having thus chosen our course, without guile and with pure purpose, let us renew our trust in God, and go forward without fear and with manly hearts."

At the outbreak of the Civil War, Dr. Robert W. Hazlett served as a surgeon of the 2nd Regiment, Virginia Volunteer Infantry. In the fall of 1862, he was appointed surgeon of Latham's independent brigade, and in 1863 he was appointed as one of the surgeons of the United States general hospital at Grafton. At the close of the war, Dr. Hazlett returned to Wheeling to practice medicine. *(Friends of Wheeling)*

October 1861

By Jeanne Finstein

"We are surrounded here by traitors," wrote Edward M. Norton on September 5, 1861, to U.S. Attorney General Edward Bates. Since the previous winter, Norton had watched with dismay as Wheeling men joined the Confederate cause, either by enlisting in the army or being elected to the Confederate Congress. In early August, the U.S. Congress had passed the Confiscation Act of 1861, permitting the takeover of property being used to benefit the Confederacy. By writing to the Attorney General, Norton was seeking assurance that he could put that law into effect in Wheeling without exceeding his legal power.

Norton and his two brothers had moved to Wheeling from Pennsylvania in 1847 and had established the Top Mill, one of the early iron mills in the city. He had been a delegate to the Chicago Convention, which nominated Abraham Lincoln for President, and afterwards was appointed to the position of U.S. Marshal. It was in that role that Norton wrote his letter. Apparently the response to the letter was positive, since Norton quickly began going after property owned by Confederate sympathizers.

In late September 1861 he seized a pair of bay horses owned by Wheeling attorney Charles Wells Russell. One of Wheeling's most distinguished lawyers, Russell is remembered as having been the attorney who argued the Wheeling Bridge Case before the U.S. Supreme Court when Pittsburgh sought to have the Suspension Bridge removed. Russell also had been at the forefront of ensuring that the Baltimore & Ohio Railroad arrived at Wheeling as its Ohio River destination. Bridge engineer Charles Ellet was his major ally. But Russell's sympathies were with the South. By the fall of 1861, he had already left Wheeling and eventually served for four years as a member of the Confederate Congress from Virginia.

On October 26, 1861, Norton seized Russell's house at 75 12th Street, under the same law. That house, which still stands, was later used as headquarters for General William Rosecrans and his staff of the Army of Western Virginia.

Norton next went after the property of another well-known Wheeling citizen. On October 31 he confiscated the home of Dr. Matthew Houston, located "on 4th between Union and Monroe" (now known as Chapline Street, between 11th and 12th Streets). Dr. Houston was one of the founders of Wheeling Hospital and one of the most prominent doctors in town. He had already left town and later served as a surgeon in the Confederate Army.

Norton's zeal against Confederates didn't stop with confiscating property. On October 6, 1861, he arrested Ellie Poole, a teacher at the Fourth Ward School in East Wheeling, "upon information which led him to believe that the lady was engaged in some treasonable correspondence." Feigning illness, Ellie was allowed to remain under guard in her home at 82 Clay Street (now18th Street). During the night she escaped and fled down river, and her amazing saga continued. She traveled by steamboat to Cincinnati and then on to Louisville. There, she found that the well-known detective Delos "Yankee" Bligh was pursuing her. Seeking to elude Bligh, Ellie boarded a train headed for Vincennes, Indiana. Bligh boarded the same train, however, and arrested Ellie. She is said to have had some $7500 in Confederate money with her – a very considerable amount for that time. Bligh took her back to Louisville and brought her before General William T. Sherman. From there, Ellie was sent to Washington, DC, where she was placed under house arrest with the infamous Rose Greenhow and several other women accused of spying for the Confederacy. While in "Greenhow Prison," Ellie and another detainee reportedly amused themselves with "fainting fits" and enjoyed the attention – and brandy – brought by the guards.

After a few months under house arrest, Ellie reluctantly signed a loyalty oath and went to Lynchburg, Virginia. There she met her future husband, a Confederate soldier, and spent the rest of her life. When the official reports of the war were compiled years later, a section on the issue of Lincoln's suspension of habeas corpus mentioned Ellie Poole by name and referred to her arrest as being justified because she was a "shrewd and dangerous spy."

Union fervor was strong in Wheeling throughout October and the rest of the year. The men who had enlisted for three-month service had mustered out in August, and most had almost immediately reenlisted for three more years. Wives, mothers, and sweethearts prepared elaborate dinners for departing soldiers. Meanwhile, "sesesh" prisoners were paraded on their way from the Island to winter confinement in the Athenaeum, a repurposed theater on the corner of 16th and Market Streets.

Newspaper articles continued to promote the idea of a separate state and expressed disdain toward the government in Richmond. One article, for example, told of an insane woman from Ritchietown who was sent to an asylum in Columbus. "Until the asylum at Weston is completed, we shall be compelled to send all subjects to Columbus. We can't send them to Staunton [Virginia], and it wouldn't do to send them there, if we could. The people down there are all crazy."

The newspapers of the day also reported disapproval of soldiers who blocked the sidewalk, forcing pedestrians to walk in the muddy street. And drunkenness among the soldiers reached such a level that city council passed an ordinance forbidding the sale of alcohol to anyone in uniform.

Toward the end of October, an article reported that three local wagon-makers – Busby, Little & Co; Joshua Bodley; and Moffit & McNabb – were hired by the federal government to make wagons and ambulances, and Washington Cline was reported to be busy forging chains for government service.

On a lighter note, another article from the October 1861 *Intelligencer* reported an improvement in ladies' hooped skirts. A greatly increased number of standards, placed closely around bottom of the skirt, reportedly made it harder for a heel to catch in the skirt, "adding much to the general strength and durability." The article noted that the idea had originated with a woman "of course" and that hooped skirts had now reached perfection.

Marshal Edward M. Norton confiscated this home of noted Wheeling attorney Charles Wells Russell, enforcing the Union's Confiscation Act. Russell had left Wheeling to serve in the Confederate government in Richmond. The house became the headquarters for General William Rosecrans when he was stationed in Wheeling. *(Photo by Jeanne Finstein)*

November 1861

By Jeanne Finstein

News relating to the Civil War dominated space in the Wheeling *Daily Intelligencer* in November 1861. First-hand reports from soldiers in the field were featured on many of the front pages, and official news reports of battle results were also included.

A front-page advertisement appeared daily for Dr. Alfred Hughes, homeopathic physician, despite the fact that he had been arrested for treason in August for failing to take the oath of allegiance. After serving some eight months in Camp Chase, he was later exchanged for another prominent doctor and moved with his family to Richmond, where one of his patients was Mrs. Robert E. Lee. Reports also stated that Alexander "Bloody" Poole of East Wheeling, perhaps related to teacher Ellie Poole, was reportedly arrested for the murder of a fellow member of the guerilla Snake Hunters.

The Sprigg House hotel was converted into a military hospital mid month and was soon filled to overflowing by convalescing soldiers, many of whom were reportedly recovering from typhoid or dysentery. Dr. Griswold was named manager of the hospital, with Dr. John Frissell appointed chief surgeon. "Supposing that there will be three hundred patients in the institution, two matrons and forty nurses will be required. The nurses must be middle aged ladies, and of undoubted character. Dr. Griswold has had numerous applications from young and interesting women, who want to act as nurses, all of which he has refused." Clemency Shelly, age 33, and Margret Crampton, age 23, were among the women selected. Shelly later received a pension for her work; Crampton did not.

Other area women also did their part in aiding the patients. The Sanitary Commission reported donations from Wheeling and surrounding areas, such as those mentioned on November 18 from Mrs. Andrew Glass: "2 comforts, 1 quilt, 1 pillow, 6 pillow cases, 2 pillow ticks, 2 towels, 2 sheets, 2 bottles wine, 1 jar apple butter, 2 tumblers jelly." The Ladies Union Aid Society also donated shirts, socks, hats, and other items for use by the soldiers at the Camp Carlile training center on Wheeling Island.

National news included the beginnings of reports of what came to be known as the "Trent Affair." This diplomatic crisis erupted after the captain of a Union ship ordered the arrest of two Confederate envoys, James Mason and John Slidell, who were sailing to Europe aboard a British mail ship, the *Trent*, to seek support for the South in the war. The British were outraged and claimed that the seizure of a neutral ship by the U.S. Navy was a violation of international law. President Abraham Lincoln's administration eventually released the men and avoided an armed conflict with Britain.

Perhaps the most important news during the month involved the beginning of the Wheeling convention during which the new state's Constitution was written. The group met beginning on November 26. Ohio County had four representatives at that convention: merchant James W. Paxton, banker Daniel Lamb, Methodist minister Gordon Battelle, and teacher Andrew F. Ross from West Liberty.

One of the first items to be addressed was that of the name of the new state. Kanawha had been suggested and had been approved by the voters. And a November 15 article in the *Intelligencer* noted that a well-known citizen of Wheeling had received mail from England addressed to him in Wheeling, Ohio County, State of Kanawha, U.S.A. However, delegates argued against the name, in part because a county and two rivers already had that name and also because some residents found the name difficult to spell. After a lengthy debate, the name West Virginia was selected.

Another debate involved the boundaries of the state. Forty-four of the current counties of West Virginia were initially included. Six others – Pendleton, Hardy, Hampshire, Morgan, Berkeley, and Jefferson – were later added after votes were taken by the citizens of those areas. Frederick County (Maryland) was also included in the potential list; apparently those citizens declined. [The remaining five counties that make up the total of West Virginia's current 55 were formed after the Civil War through division from existing counties.] The state was also to include "so much of the bed, banks, and shores of the Ohio River as heretofore appertained to the State of Virginia."

The newspaper noted that the new state would contain more white people than the State of South Carolina, "which has played so important a part for evil in the history of the country." The article then listed the populations of the 39 counties that were then considered to be included, with a total population of 281,768. The population of Ohio County was given as 22,422, making it by far the most populous county in the state.

The most controversial issue during the convention was slavery, with delegates ranging from slave owners to abolitionists. Rev. Battelle called for a ban on the importation of slaves into the new state and for gradual emancipation. An eventual compromise provided that no African-Americans, whether free or slave, could enter the state. The U.S. Congress later required different provisions on slavery as a condition of admission of West Virginia to the Union, with slave children born after July 4, 1863, to be freed, and slave minors to be freed upon their 21st birthdays. By the time West Virginia was officially a state, adult slaves in the rest of Virginia had already been freed by the Emancipation Proclamation.

The *Intelligencer* also reported on shortages of food and clothing in the South and mentioned that whiskey and ice were scarce in Richmond. One article reported that a placard had been seen in a "fashionable drinking saloon" in Richmond that stated, "Drinks fifteen cents each. Gentlemen will please refrain from eating the ice in their tumblers after drinking." Presumably this request was intended for those customers who bought refills and not for recycling purposes.

Massachusetts native John Frissell moved to Wheeling in 1836 and set up his medical practice. He is believed to have been the first surgeon in western Virginia to use chloroform in critical operations. Soon after the Civil War began, Dr. Frissell was appointed medical superintendent of the military prisoners and soldiers stationed in Wheeling. He was also a member of the state board of examiners for surgeons entering the army during the war. *(Geography of West Virginia by Knote, A. C., 1895, courtesy of the Ohio County Public Library)*

December 1861
By Ed Phillips

The Athenaeum, which was to become an infamous Wheeling Civil War prison, was built in 1854 and came to be called "Lincoln's Bastille" by prisoners during he war. According to its owners, the building originally was to be used in conjunction with the B & O Railroad station, which was just a couple of blocks away.

Located on the southeast corner of Market and John (now 16th) Streets, the building was a three-story brick edifice with no basement, constructed with the latest technology of the time. The roof and floor beams were of cast iron and manufactured in New Jersey. The third floor of the structure was designed as a theater, with a large stage, dressing rooms for the actors, and seating on the floor and balcony. The latest heating system was installed for the comfort of the patrons. According to one of the newspaper reviewers of the time, the theater was one of the best between the Allegheny Mountains and Chicago.

The first performance was on January 27, 1855. The actors usually belonged to a traveling company with special actors brought in for a week or two to perform special shows. The evening's entertainment typically consisted of a major play, followed by a song or dance and a shorter comic play. Although Shakespeare was a perennial favorite, "Ingomar, the Barbarian" "beautiful and always a favorite," was also offered.

In April 1856 the managers tried to attract a better class of audience and provided omnibuses to take the gentry home after the performance. Police were stationed in the theater to discourage the riff-raff, and the admission charge was 50 cents for the parquette and dress circle and 25 cents for the balcony.

By November 1856 the theater was drawing large crowds, and the manager, Mr. Hanchett, booked the play "Uncle Tom's Cabin." It was shown seven days a week with a special performance on Saturday just for school children and women unable to attend the evening show. The play was sold out for most performances. Probably, the most famous actor who ever graced the Athenaeum was Edwin Booth, brother of John Wilkes Booth, who performed in January 1857. He did five shows of Shakespeare then switched to "Cardinal Richelieu," causing the local newspaper critic to devote a whole column to criticizing the performance and recommending that Booth stick to what he did best...Shakespeare.

The coming of the Civil War brought a new and drastic change to the building. Fifty secession prisoners who had been confined at Camp Carlile were moved to the Athenaeum and housed on the second floor. A large room there was converted to have a kitchen in one end with a large dining table running the entire length. Fifty bunks lined the northern wall. The first prisoners were those who had refused to take the oath of allegiance. These prisoners were only detained at the prison for a day or two until they could be sent on to Camp Chase in Columbus, Ohio. By December 1861, the prisoners numbered close to a hundred. Major Darr of General Rosecrans' staff was assigned as Provost Marshall and put in charge of the prison.

The first escape took place in April 1862, when George Deering cut a hole through the floor of the second story, lowered himself down on a makeshift rope, and just walked out the front door as there were no guards on duty. This was the first of many escape attempts, although only two or three were successful.

By late 1863, the Confederate prisoners were moved out as quickly as possible to make room for Union soldiers convicted by court martial. The federal government then took over the whole building, turning it into a permanent federal prison. Cells were constructed on the former stage, and the north side underneath the dress circle was converted for female prisoners. The south side became a hospital. A fence twenty feet high was erected around the vacant lot in back of the building that was used as an exercise block.

Judson Mazingo, a 21-year-old prisoner, died of scarlet fever in the prison hospital. By 1864, the prison hospital was so crowded it could not effectively operate; so forty-five patients were moved to the Catholic Wheeling Hospital in North Wheeling. The prison hospital was then used for the overflow of prisoners.

In order to complete the prison, a new bake house and a structure to hold fuel were constructed in the vacant lot adjacent to the building. The prison was now self-contained. The prisoners were occasionally sent to clean the streets of Wheeling and to do other work around the government buildings.

After the war the Provost Marshall ordered the prison closed, and the last prisoners were sent back to their regiments for discharge on September 27, 1865. The owners of the building filed suit against the government for damages that they claimed had occurred while in the government's possession. The suit was dismissed as the government claimed that in reality it had increased the value of the building and had paid a fair rent during its use as a prison.

In March 1867, Butterfield & Co. opened a malt storage business on the lower floor, adding a full-length basement to the building. At half past twelve on October 11, 1868, the Athenaeum caught fire. Wheeling had only one pumper capable of putting water on the third floor and roof, so the fire soon got out of control, and the building was allowed to burn itself out. The firemen instead concentrated on preventing the fire from spreading to other nearby buildings. The loss to the owner was estimated to be $150,000 and was the largest fire in Wheeling up to that time. As a direct result of this fire, Wheeling purchased more steam fire engines.

The building had a life of only 14 years, but it saw much of the cultural and Civil War history of Wheeling during this short period. The location is now a small park in front of West Virginia Northern Community College, and the Athenaeum is remembered by none.

The right side of this Civil War era sketch shows the corner of the Athenaeum. No other pictures of the building are known. *(Frank Leslie's Illustrated Newspaper, August 10, 1861)*

January 1862

By Bekah Karelis

As the bells of the First Presbyterian Church rang in the New Year on January 1, 1862, the newspaper wrote, "A Year that opened in National peace and prosperity closes in the face of the tramp and clangor of war and all its desolations. Now many brave men have fallen in battle and how much pain and anguish has been felt by the loved ones at home. What a world of solemn thought there is in all of this!" The war that had been predicted to last only three months had lasted eight months by the dawn of 1862, and no end was in sight.

At the bustling Custom House, the Constitutional Convention was a little slow to get going on the first day of the year, with only 10 persons present. They declared an informal adjournment until the following day. The month would involve debates about everything from county representation, officials' term limits, and tax policies. On January 27, Mr. Gordon Battelle first proposed gradual emancipation of slaves into their debates.

While the Convention was busy ironing out details for the new state, rumors spread far and wide about what went on within the walls of the Custom House. An account from Richmond stated, "We hear from the Pierpont dynasty at Wheeling that the bogus Virginia Convention recently in session in that town has resorted to a measure of punishment against secessionists which is without a parallel in the history of legislation. An ordinance has been adopted divorcing all refugee husbands from their wives, and all refugee wives from their husbands declaring that no citizens of Virginia can remain united in lawful matrimony to a citizen of Pierpont's Commonwealth."

Brigadier General William S. Rosecrans had arrived in Wheeling on the steamer *Prima Donna* on December 4, 1861, and took up temporary residence in Room 141 at the McLure Hotel. Rosecrans planned to spend the winter in Wheeling with his family. At the time of his arrival, he commanded all of the forces in Western Virginia. The newspaper noted, "He seems to be a man of stirring energy, with very little of the red tape about him."

His headquarters were not determined on his arrival, but the houses of C.W. Russell and E.H. Fitzhugh were under consideration. Also considered favorably, was the house of Dr. Stanton (the current Fort Henry Club), who had relocated to Mississippi the year before, but "there were difficulties considering the furnishings in the house." When a place was chosen, Rosecrans moved into the Charles Wells Russell house at 75 12th Street, which would serve as headquarters for the Army of Western Virginia for the duration of their stay in Wheeling.

William S. Rosecrans was born in Ohio and attended West Point where he began his military career. There, he roomed with James Longstreet and A.P. Stewart, both of whom would become Confederate generals. After graduation, Rosecrans began working as a civil engineer, eventually taking over mining concerns in western Virginia. When the Civil War began he was a colonel aide-de-camp to Gen. George McClellan and took part in the Battle of Rich Mountain and Corrick's Ford. He was then promoted to Major General and commanded the Army of Western Virginia.

Gen. Rosecrans' "bodyguards" of one hundred mounted men arrived on January 18, 1862. Their horses were kept in the government stables that were near the Hempfield Railroad depot.

Though a war was happening, there was still entertainment to be had in the city. The Athenaeum building, or rather the portion originally designed for theatrical purposes, was leased by a group of men from Philadelphia who planned to renovate and re-open in late January, all while there were prisoners being kept in other parts of the building, housed in rooms beneath the stage and boxes. Customers were assured that this would not affect the quality of the shows.

The citizens of the city hosted many events to fundraise for the war effort. The ladies of the 2nd Presbyterian Church hosted a supper for the Benefit of the Young Men's Christian Association to "aid them in carrying out their special objects, with a particular reference towards supplying our soldiers in Western Virginia with Bibles and Testimonials and other moral and religious reading. Also, the Ladies of the Union Aid Society gave a supper at Washington Hall where Gen. Rosecrans made an appearance with a portion of his staff in full dress uniform to support their efforts.

Soldiers were daily arriving or moving through the city. On January 14, 1862, one hundred infirm soldiers arrived from Romney and were housed in the Sprigg House Hospital. Also mentioned in the January newspaper was ambulance production. "Busbey, Little and Hays are making about one hundred ambulances for the army. The ambulances are to be drawn by two horses and by four, the old two wheeled one horse vehicles, having been weighed in the balance and found wanting. The ambulances manufactured by this firm are of the very best material and are not excelled in finish or durability. Gen. Rosecrans has pronounced them the very thing."

Three thousand soldiers crossed the river from Bellaire to Benwood, one regiment at a time. One particular regiment of soldiers was quartered in Benwood, detained on their journey to Patterson's Creek near Cumberland. The river was quickly rising due to heavy rains, and the soldiers watched as the residents of Benwood abandoned their homes along the river to seek higher ground. After the residents had left, the soldiers, unaware of the reason why the homes were being vacated, moved themselves into the houses and soon had the "fires burning up again brightly and cheerfully." They lay down on their newfound beds, and fell asleep. By 2:00 a.m. they were awoken by "Water, water everywhere. Some clambered upon the roofs of the houses, others gained foot-holds upon the window sills, and such another yelling for lifeboats, steamboats, skiffs, planks, and water crafts of all sorts, was never heard. The boys were finally all rescued safely."

The Wheeling – or "Rosecrans" – ambulance was designed by General William Rosecrans when he was stationed in Wheeling and was mass-produced by local carriage makers. Beginning with the Battle of Antietam, it was used extensively during the Civil War. It was furnished inside with padded seats for eight, convertible into beds for two. It was simple in construction, easily kept in repair, and in many of the divisions of the Army of the Potomac, it survived the war after participating in every campaign. *(Medical and Surgical History of the War of the Rebellion – Part Third – Surgical Volume – Surgeon General's Office – Washington, DC)*

By Margaret Brennan

Even as the observance of Black History Month has concluded for another year, it might be well to focus on slavery and the Civil War era, especially as it relates to Wheeling.

In March of 1861, Alexander Stephens, vice president of the Confederate States of America, pointed out, "... our peculiar institution African slavery as it exists amongst us ... was the immediate cause of the late rupture." Bob Sutton, chief historian for the National Park Service stated, "Slavery was the principal cause of the Civil War, period." There were other important and contributing issues, but slavery was at the core of the rending of the Union.

Some of the founding fathers and mothers of Wheeling were enslaved, as we know the history of Ebenezer Zane's slave, "Daddy Sam," and "Aunt Rachel," another Zane slave who lived to be over 100 years old. The Zane wills are chilling as they bequeath slaves as they do their household goods. Probably the largest number of enslaved in Wheeling belonged to Lydia Shepherd Cruger who, in the 1850 census, owned 13 slaves, including Israel, Jack, Susan, and Mandy, a five-year-old.

Wheeling as we know it during the Civil War was divided in its loyalties. The upper class gentry often had feeling for "old Virginia." Thus, we see names such as Zane, Hughes, Moore, Goshorn, Steenrod, and Phillips on the "traitors" list. Often these families owned slaves, usually domestic servants who tended the house, helped rear the children, did the cooking, and drove the carriage. There is evidence today of this life in the slave galleries of two local churches, First Presbyterian on Chapline Street and old St. Matthew's Episcopal on Byron Street. There the slave benches, set against the gallery back wall so as not to be seen from the main body, put us in touch with those tragic times.

In 1860, the population of Wheeling was 14,100, and the slave population of Ohio County, with no separation for Wheeling, was 100, with 42 males and 58 females. There were also free black males and females among the citizens. Wheeling was part of the social and political fabric of slaveholding Virginia. Knowing this and the city's key location in terms of the National Road and the Ohio River, it is not unexpected that there would be a flourishing slave auction block here, located at the north end of the Second Ward market house on 10th Street.

Thomas B. Seabright, in his history of the National Road, wrote, "Negro slaves were frequently seen on the National Road. They were driven over the road arranged in couples and fashioned to a long, thick rope, or cable, like horses." Joseph Bell, born in 1819, remembered seeing on Wheeling streets "gangs of slaves chained together, women as well as men, on their way south. As a little boy, I remember standing on the sidewalk with my brother when such as gang was passing. We were eating an ear of corn apiece, which some of the slaves begged from us."

The market bell would ring, announcing the slave auction. It is vividly described in the book *Bonnie Belmont* by Judge John Cochran. In 1855 he wrote, "It was a wooden movable platform about two and a half feet high and six feet square, approached by some three or four steps. The auctioneer was a little dapper fellow with a ringing voice. Not a very large crowd was surrounding the auction block. On top of it was a portly and rather aged negress and the auctioneer."

In December 1858, the Wheeling newspaper reported, "Five negro girls ... were sold last week for one thousand dollars each." Many of the slaves auctioned at Wheeling were bought by agents for plantations in the deep south and as they say were "sold down the river" for back-breaking work in the cotton fields. Others might find themselves in the Kanawha Salines near Charleston, at its peak employing 3,140 slaves to extract the pure red salt.

One of the more well known slave stories of Wheeling concerned Sara Lucy Bagby. She was purchased by John Goshorn for $600 in January 1852 in Richmond, Virginia, and in 1857 she was given to John's son, William. In 1860, Lucy escaped to Cleveland, where she became a maid at the home of A.G. Riddle, a congressman-elect. It became politically expedient for him to send Lucy to work for a jeweler friend, L.A. Benton.

Apparently someone in Cleveland alerted William Goshorn to Lucy's whereabouts, and he traveled to the city and contacted the U.S. marshal, demanding her return. The marshal took Lucy into custody. At her hearing the next day, January 20, 1861, large crowds gathered. Lucy's case was postponed for two days while evidence was gathered, and she was held in the post office building, a twin to West Virginia Independence Hall.

It was proven that she was indeed the property of William Goshorn, so under the 1850 Fugitive Slave Law, she had to be returned to Wheeling and her owner. The people of Cleveland raised almost $1,200 to buy her freedom, but Goshorn would not hear of it.

Getting Lucy Bagby out of Cleveland was no small feat, as many wanted her to be rescued, even by force. The sheriff swore in 150 new deputies who escorted Lucy and her owner to the train, and she was returned safely to Wheeling, only to be placed in jail. After a few days, she was sent to Charleston to stay with Goshorn relatives until things quieted down.

Lucy was eventually freed and went to Pittsburgh where she married George Johnson, a former soldier in the Union Army. She and her husband relocated to Cleveland where Lucy worked as a cook and house servant for the leading families. It is said that she came back to Wheeling to visit William Goshorn before he died in 1891.

Lucy, formally Lucinda, died of septicemia on July 14, 1906, at about 63 years of age. She is buried in Woodland Cemetery in Cleveland and had an unmarked grave until recently, when a bene-factor donated a gravestone. Lucy is considered the last fugitive slave returned under the 1850 law.

As Abraham Lincoln noted in 1864, "If slavery is not wrong,

nothing is wrong." Sara Lucinda Bagby Johnson and her fellow enslaved in Wheeling and elsewhere testify to this truth.

Prior to the Civil War, slaves were one of the largest exports of Virginia. Some slaves were sold in Wheeling at a slave market located on the north end of the Second Ward Market. A commemorative plaque on 10th Street now stands near the site. *(Ohio County Public Library Archives)*

March 1862

By Kate Quinn

One of the city's unsung Civil War heroes is Jesse Reno, born in Wheeling, Va., on April 20, 1823. Jesse was the third oldest of eight children born to Lewis and Rebecca Quinby Reno and lived in our city until he was 7, when his family moved to Franklin, Pennsylvania. His ancestors had changed the family name from Reynault to Reno when they immigrated to this country in the 1700s.

Reno attended West Point where he became friends with Thomas "Stonewall" Jackson. Other classmates included George McClellan. He graduated eighth in his class and was soon fighting in the Mexican-American War. He was seriously injured at the Battle of Chapultapec. After that war, he taught mathematics at West Point and instructed in the use of the howitzer. After conducting a road survey in Minnesota, he married and had five children. His son, Conrad, became a Boston attorney and writer. His son, Jesse W., is known for inventing the first escalator.

Reno was known as a "soldier's soldier" and though young led his men bravely. During the Civil War, it became imperative to stop General Robert E. Lee's advance through the Blue Ridge Mountains of Maryland. South Mountain presented quite an obstacle to Gen. McClellan's troops, so he divided his army into three units in an attempt to cross it. Lee's plans (known as Order 191) detailing troop movements fell into Union hands, and McClellan was able to position his soldiers at the three gaps in the mountain where Lee's men were entrenched but badly outnumbered.

Union General Ambrose Burnside, whose second in command by request was Jesse Reno, now a brigadier general, commanded the right wing of troops. At 9 a.m. September 14, 1862, the armies clashed. Lt. Col. Rutherford B. Hayes (later to be elected President) was severely wounded. The exhausted Union troops were overwhelmed by reinforcements of Confederate soldiers who spread out around the Daniel Wise farm. Reno was shot by a North Carolina sharpshooter as he stood in front of his troops, his uniform as general an easy target. After the battle, Union men dumped the bodies of 60 Confederates down the well of farmer Wise and paid him $60 in compensation.

Although an important boost to Northern morale, South Mountain saw the death of 2,325 Union men of 28,000 and 2,685 of 18,000 Confederate troops.

After he was shot, Reno was taken by stretcher to the command post of Gen. Samuel Sturgis where he said, "Hello, Sam. I'm dead." His voice was so strong that Sturgis replied that things could not be as bad as all that, yet minutes later Reno stated, "Yes, yes, I'm dead – good-bye!" and passed on. Other historians say that his last words were, "Tell my command that if not in body, I will be with them in spirit."

Jesse Reno is buried at Oak Hill Cemetery in Georgetown, Washington, D.C. He was just 39 years old. Some say his body was wrapped in the famous flag that belonged to Barbara Fritchie, of the noble poem by John Greenleaf Whittier, which extolled Confederate soldiers passing through Fredericksburg to "Shoot if you must this old gray head, but spare your country's flag, she said." The poem is a myth, as Fritchie was 90 years old and bedridden at the time the troops passed through her town, and they did not come within 1,000 yards of her door.

The town of Reno, Nev., was named for Jesse Reno, who was admired by the town's sponsor, Charles Crocker, who liked the sound of the name and admired the soldier as a hero. Reno's statue stands in that town.

Wheeling native and career officer Jesse Reno served in the Mexican-American War prior to the Civil War. He attained the rank of Major General but was killed during the battle of South Mountain in 1862, age 39. *(Library of Congress)*

April 1862
By Seán P. Duffy

In April 1862, one year to the month after Fort Sumter fell, Wheeling found herself the capital city of loyal Virginia with Governor Francis Pierpont installed in the Custom House. Soldiers and civilians jostled each other in busy streets, alternately dusty or muddy depending on rainfall. While members of the Fourth Regiment, Virginia Militia assembled at street corners to elect officers, the Mountain Department's chief quartermaster placed ads seeking 1500 strong horses and 2000 mules. Suitable animals were assigned to Captain Frank Buell, commander of the First Virginia Volunteer Artillery, better known as the "Pierpont Battery," who took them to Wheeling Island to be trained to "conduct themselves in a fight."

The B&O Railroad between Wheeling and Baltimore, a vital artery for troops and supplies, was reopened after bridges damaged by rebel "bushwackers" were repaired and troops had been committed to protecting the route. To celebrate the arrival of the first passenger train from Baltimore, the Pierpont Battery fired a 100-gun salute.

Gen. William Rosecrans, who had been headquartered in Wheeling since December, left for Washington. While he was still at the McLure, his officers expressed their sentiments, promising to "forever honor him as the man, the soldier, and the Christian." Gen. John C. Fremont's staff arrived on April 6.

Despite the increasing ubiquity of the war, Wheeling's civilians persevered. The town remained home to an array of retail establishments selling everything from cigars and snuff to Ayer's Sarsaparilla for purifying the blood; from jeans and hoop skirts to horse buckets and "Jenny Lind keelers" (tubs for butter-making). At Washington Hall, where the opening session of the Second Wheeling Convention that eventually established the Restored Government of Virginia had met, the celebrated cantatrice, Madame Anna Bishop, performed. Across the Ohio River, a pack of twenty or more well bred hounds followed by nattily clad men on horseback could often be seen chasing foxes toward the river.

At mid-month, U.S. Senator John Carlile, the vocal unionist and driving force behind the establishment of the Restored Government, got into a well-publicized fistfight with U.S. Marshal Norton outside Merchant's and Mechanic's Bank. "The two distinguished gentlemen," the *Daily Intelligencer* reported, "clinched and proceeded to strike and wool one another [until] they were separated." Inspired more by pugilist "Young Sam" Scranton, who started a boxing school on Main Street, than by Senator Carlile's unseemly street brawling, a "Wheeling Gymnasium" was created on the second floor of Paxton's Row, for men who desired invigorating exercise – some "German Turnerism."

It had been less than two months since delegates in convention at the Custom House had unanimously approved a constitution for the proposed new state. On April 3, the document was submitted to the people of Virginia's western counties, who overwhelmingly approved by a vote of 18,862 to 514. In Ohio County the vote was 1023 for and 31 against.

Included on the same ballot was the controversial issue of the gradual emancipation of slaves – the "Free State" question. The *Intelligencer* came out in favor of the concept as an expedient step for the admission of West Virginia, lest "all our efforts...prove a splendid farce and we shall be under the rule of the rebels of the east." The people of Wheeling resoundingly agreed, voting in favor 617 to 29. South Wheeling was especially adamant, approving 129 to 2. "Ritchietown always covers herself with glory," the *Intelligencer* crowed. "She is the greatest state in the Union – She voted right up to handle yesterday on the Free State question."

The Athenaeum, Wheeling's theater turned makeshift military prison, was packed to capacity with suspected bushwackers, traitors, and spies. Visible from the south-facing windows of the Custom House where the new constitution had recently been drafted, the Athenaeum was, at best, a prison of dubious security. In late March, an inmate aptly named Swindler, on the pretense of "using the privy" (inexplicably located outside prison walls) duped a guard and escaped. Prisoner Swayne's escape a few days later reads like a Keystone Cops script. Exploiting the established gullibility of the guards, Swayne feigned sickness and jumped from the roof leaving his shoes atop the now infamous privy, "so the soldiers might have something by which to remember him." He "struck out for the Hempfield Railroad in his stocking feet," stopping at the home of a Mr. Britt who, inexplicably, fed him breakfast. Swayne was eating when a guard arrived. Snatching the guard's rifle, Swayne shot and missed. The guard returned fire with his revolver, missing both shots at the fleeing fugitive. Britt then grabbed his squirrel rifle and pursued Swayne, caught him and returned him to the Athenaeum where he was "bucked and gagged."

Other "secession sympathizers" were imprisoned for singing "treasonable songs" or denouncing the Wheeling Government. By late April, the Athenaeum had become so overcrowded with real and imagined enemies of the state that inmates were regularly hauled away to Camp Chase.

The disloyalty paranoia was evident in the multitude of federal court proceedings involving accused traitors. Both Fremont and Pierpont committed themselves to punishing disloyalty. "A rigid censorship" was to be instituted "in all the counties over which the Wheeling Government has jurisdiction." Anyone in a licensed business, including physicians, dentists, bankers, and keepers of toll bridges was required to recite the Oath of Allegiance (and to mean it).

Regarding the war itself, the newspapers almost daily printed letters received from "our Wheeling boys" at various fronts. The town was still abuzz with news of the recent skirmishing near Winchester, where many Wheeling men were fighting with the loyal First Virginia against Stonewall Jackson's Confederate forces in what would become known in military legend as the Shenandoah Valley Campaign.

Wheeling businessman Augustus Pollack – who had recently

opened a notion and fancy goods store on Main Street – translated, for the *Intelligencer*, a vivid letter from a fellow German immigrant serving in the First Virginia. "The stoutest heart is awestricken by the appalling spectacle on a battle field at night, the former uninterrupted stillness of sleeping nature...changed to the theatre where unfortunate beings, mangled and crippled, are stretched on the ground dampened by their late blood, with wounds wide open, groaning, wailing, helpless, evoking a kind Creator to terminate their existence."

Another Wheeling soldier reported that twenty-seven "Shriver Grays," – a Confederate regiment composed largely of Wheeling men – had been killed or captured at Winchester. Among the dead was William Robertson, whose two brothers fought for the Union in the same battle. "As soon as the two loyal boys heard of the death of their brother William," the *Intelligencer* reported, "they pushed on to the house where he was lying. But soldiers were in the act of burying him."

April 1862 also saw the horrific carnage of the battle known in the North as Pittsburg Landing and in the South as Shiloh. On April 6, Confederate forces under Generals P.G.T. Beauregard and Joseph Johnston attacked Union forces under General Ulysses S. Grant at Shiloh, Tennessee. Grant's army was nearly defeated. But a quote making the rounds in the newspapers provided the epilogue, "Beauregard's 'victory' at Pittsburg Landing is...like that described by 'John Phoenix.'...'I held the enemy down by my nose, which I had inserted between his teeth for that purpose.'"

The federals rallied when reinforcements arrived, and the tide turned. Drained by their efforts, the Union troops failed to pursue the retreating Confederates. Shiloh was a bloodbath: 13,000 of 63,000 Union and 11,000 of 40,000 Confederate troops were killed or wounded.

Major William Wallace of Martinsville (Martins Ferry) commanded the 15th Ohio, mostly Belmont County troops, at Pittsburg

Landing. "He [Wallace] was everywhere conspicuous on the bloody field," a soldier wrote, "and always in the thickest of the fray." Numerous Martinsville soldiers were killed in the battle.

The chaplain of 78th Ohio wrote poignantly to his uncle in Wheeling, "The vast armies dashed against each other as two angry thunder clouds...But oh the horrid battlefield after the battle. Think of from 5000 to 6000 of our fellow men scattered like leaves all over the ground in every imaginable position and condition, cold in death...think of a vast body of men dead, dying, mangled, bleeding and wailing and you have the results of our great battle." A captain in the chaplain's brigade was devastated to recognize one of the dead rebels as his brother. "Overwhelming was the tide of anguish as it roiled over the surviving brother's heart." A father who enlisted with his two sons found them both dead side-by-side on the field. "Long did he sit and gaze upon his dead and sigh." A German regiment of the 58th Ohio lost nearly 100 men. "A large German stood over a fellow soldier whose face was horribly mangled by a cannonball...and continued to say in broken English, 'He was my best friend. He was my best friend.'"

As April turned to May the Pierpont Battery marched down Main Street to board a B&O train that would take them to Franklin Virginia to join Gen. John C. Fremont. As the troops passed a shoe house near the suspension bridge, a woman of "secesh persuasion" pulled an American flag out of a window, sparking outrage. Unfazed, the battery marched on, presenting, as the *Intelligencer* beamed, "a very warlike appearance as it moved through the streets."

West Point graduate William Rosecrans had a career as a civil engineer before the war. "Old Rosy" attained the rank of Major General during the war. While stationed in Wheeling, he designed an innovative ambulance that helped save many wounded soldiers. He was for a time considered as a vice presidential running mate for President Lincoln in the 1864 election. In later years he served as a U.S. Congressman from California. *(Library of Congress)*

May 1862

By Jeanne Finstein

During the month of May 1862, the Wheeling *Daily Intelligencer* was filled with news of the war and related events in Wheeling. Articles included frequent reports on prisoners coming to the Athenaeum or leaving it to be taken to Camp Chase in Columbus. Most of the prisoners were charged with offenses such as "bushwhacking, uttering seditious sentiments," aiding rebels, or failure to sign the oath of allegiance. Some were described as "miserable specimens of humanity" and "degenerate Virginians of a lower order."

Also lodged in the Athenaeum in May was a "secession Amazon," a young woman from Braxton County named Mary Jane Green. She had been arrested before and charged with "carrying her skirts full of letters to the rebel army," had been released upon a "solemn pledge to sin no more," but was then charged with destroying a telegraph line built by the Federal army.

The beginning of the month saw the departure from Wheeling of General John C. Fremont, who had been staying with his family for five weeks in the confiscated home of a Mr. Stanton, a southern sympathizer, at the corner of Fourth and Quincy Streets (now Chapline and 12th and known as the Fort Henry Club). Despite fears based on attacks on Fremont in Congress and in the press, citizens of Wheeling were favorably impressed with the General. They reported that his wife shared in his labors and were amused by his young son Frank, who always appeared in a uniform complete with sword and had "an insane hankering after confections."

Toward the end of the month, local authorities began to arrest area residents who were considered secessionists. Among them were William W. Boggs; William Goshorn; M.F. Hullihen; well-known clothier Thomas Hughes and his brother Alfred Hughes, a homeopathic doctor; and Judge George W. Thompson. Those arrested were required to take the oath of allegiance to support the Constitution of the United States and the restored Government of Virginia as a condition of their release. None signed, and Judge Thompson, despite claiming to be a Unionist, stated that the "restored Government exists in violation of the Constitution of the United States and that being required to take the two oaths together violates the one in assuming the other."

Reports from Charleston included results of Court Martial proceedings held there. Private John W. Gray of the 2nd Virginia Cavalry was charged with "writing a false and abusive letter to Governor Peirpoint [as his name was then spelled] and using insulting language to his company commander." He was dishonorably discharged. Two officers in the 1st Virginia Cavalry were charged with keeping their wives in camp dressed in the uniforms of soldiers, along with other offenses including drunkenness and playing cards with privates. Both were dismissed from the service. Seven soldiers from the 45th Ohio Volunteers were charged with mutiny. All but one were sentenced "to be taken in chains to the Dry Tortugas...and there kept at hard labor, with ball and chain attached to the left ankle, for the term of 18 months."

A local man saw action for the Confederacy in mid month. Marshall County native Francis L. Hoge, a U.S. Naval Academy graduate, was on board the USS Susquehanna in the Mediterranean when the war broke out. Upon returning to the country, Hoge resigned from the U.S. Navy and entered the Confederate Navy. He was with a group patrolling the James River and took part in the Battle of Drewry's Bluff on May 15, 1862. At the time, the Federal fleet was attempting to come up the James to Richmond, and the Confederates were determined they wouldn't get there, blocking the river with debris and mounting guns on the bluff. Hoge served with distinction in command of the gun that was nearest the enemy. The battle disabled the USS Galena and engaged the ironclad Monitor. Confederate shells couldn't pierce her heavy armor, but she proved ineffective in the battle – her guns couldn't go high enough to reach the elevated batteries. Three other Union ships either withdrew or stayed out of range. Richmond, just 7 miles away, remained safe.

Frequent reports on activities of the First Virginia Infantry, along with occasional letters from soldiers, also appeared in the paper. There was speculation that since the regiment consisted of the first loyal Virginians to cross the Blue Ridge Mountains, they might also be the first to enter Richmond, along with the "grand army of McClellan." The capture of Richmond, of course, was not soon to come. Letters printed in the *Intelligencer* from soldiers in the field included one from Zekel Hardy who stated, "I am so happy to see that this wicked and unholy war is cumin to a klose fastly...I like Freemont's plan – 'total anniherlashin & utter Xtermunashin' ...its the only wa bi which this thing kin be squashed."

A more literate letter was published from a Wheeling boy, identified only as Orloff, describing conditions in a military hospital. "You ask what is going on there?" he writes. "Just inside the tent you see a man lying on a pallet of straw, suffering the most excruciating pain from a wound received probably a month ago. The surgeon is about to perform the painful operation of amputating one of his legs...The dull grating of the saw as it is drawn back and forth through the bone of a human leg is more than the ear of a common feeling man can bear. Over yonder in the old church is another sight far from pleasant. The seats of the church have been removed, and in their stead are placed upwards of fifty rude bunks, on each of which lies a sick soldier, apparently in the last stage of some fatal disease...The average deaths here are about two every twenty-four hours...There is a great lack of nurses...If there was better care taken of the sick there would not be half so many deaths."

On a lighter note, the paper reported that Mrs. President Lincoln had purchased her new spring hat in Troy, NY, that the Empress Eugenie had adopted a new style of petticoat in Paris, and that the Wheeling Female Seminary had given a "very pleasant and successful" party with handsome decorations. More ominously, the newspaper also included an advertisement for an "elegant black dress, intended for slight mourning." Unfortunately, many women in Wheeling would find more need for that garment than for a fancy hat or petticoat.

Francis Hoge is pictured as a young man in his U.S. Navy uniform. When the war began, he left the Union forces and joined the Confederate Navy, serving with distinction. In later years, Hoge served as the city engineer for Wheeling and was responsible for the building of the stone Main Street Bridge. *(Photo courtesy of Larry Evans, great, great nephew of Francis Hoge)*

June 1862
By Judi Hendrickson

As the Civil War continued into its second summer and local men fought in places far from Wheeling, efforts were being made by others closer to home to formalize statehood for West Virginia. Two men, Waitman T. Willey of Morgantown and John S. Carlile of Clarksburg, had been elected to the United States Senate to represent the Restored Government of Virginia and had key roles in the formation of the new state.

During the month of June 1862, Willey presented a memorandum to the United States Senate to create a new state. The memorandum was referred to the Committee on Territories, where Carlisle drafted the first version of the statehood bill for West Virginia. This version included fifteen additional counties in the Shenandoah Valley, the gradual emancipation of slaves, and a new state constitutional convention. The Senators immediately offered revisions to the bill that called for immediate emancipation.

On July 1, 1862, U.S. Senator Willey proposed a compromise West Virginia statehood bill, subsequently known as the Willey Amendment, which established gradual slave emancipation and removed fifteen Shenandoah Valley counties. On July 14 the West Virginia statehood bill passed through the U.S. Senate, thanks to the Willey Amendment. Carlile's vote against the bill made him a traitor in the eyes of many West Virginians, and he was never again elected to political office.

The *Daily Intelligencer* reported that rebel prisoner Dr. Herjoy, accused of being a rebel spy, was brought to Wheeling from Clarksburg and put in custody of the Provost Marshal, Major Darr. Herjoy had served as a surgeon in the rebel army and was arrested in Clarksburg.

On June 5 The Provost Marshal Major Darr received an order from headquarters instructing him to send the secessionists, Judge George W. Thompson; Dr. Alfred Hughes, a homeopathic physician practicing in Wheeling; and William Goshorn, a Wheeling merchant, to Camp Chase, near Columbus, Ohio, where they would be kept until they gave some evidence of loyalty. After serving 8 months, Dr. Alfred Hughes was released. He and his wife and children returned to Wheeling where he closed his practice, sold his home, and was granted permission by Secretary of War Edwin Stanton to move to Richmond. Because of Hughes' connections with several federal generals, his family was allowed to transport not only themselves, but also their 13 trunks of luggage, at a time when getting only a bundle transported was nearly impossible.

Hughes' arrival in Richmond accompanied by the unusual amount of baggage gave rise to a rumor that he was a commissioner of peace sent by the United States Government, giving him much power until the end of the war. He again opened a homeopathic practice; among his patients during and after the war was the wife of General Robert E. Lee. Hughes was later elected to the Legislature of Virginia and remained a member until the fall of Richmond. He was an advocate of the enlistment of slaves in the Southern ranks. After the war, he moved from Richmond to Baltimore.

The *Intelligencer* reported that Perry Hays and a man named Silcot, two notorious guerrillas who had been marauding throughout Calhoun and adjoining counties for a year, were brought to Wheeling in charge of Capt. Baggs. They came into the Union camp under the armistice granted by Col. Rathbone, and in view of that fact, it was not yet determined what would be done with them.

Stragglers from Colonel Mulligan's Regiment were left in Wheeling. Some of the young soldiers got into trouble with a Benwood tavern keeper named Sullivan, who had been selling them whisky. A fight broke out, during which Sullivan was badly beaten. Colonel Mulligan had previously given a general warning in reference to this matter, so when the fight occurred, the whisky in Sullivan's establishment was destroyed. The men were arrested and sent to the Athenaeum.

Some other interesting things were also going on in Wheeling at the time. It was reported that 14 ladies whose husbands were in the habit of spending too much money at a saloon went into the establishment, destroyed its contents, smashed bottles and glasses, and poured whiskey into the gutters. Their husbands were fined $1.00 each for the destruction. Several young ladies volunteered as army nurses but were reportedly rejected because of their good looks. And in Moundsville, a farmer ordered a post mortem on his dead cow, resulting in the discovery of eight very tiny, fully formed calves inside.

Ads placed in the *Intelligencer* were plentiful. A.M. Adams, Merchant Tailor, 36 Water Street, offered made-to-order, at the shortest notice uniforms for officers of the U.S. Army. Cooper and Bushels offered Mourning Clothing including Lupens Bombazine cloth and black silk. And an advertisement for 100 good artillery horses 15-1/2 to 16 hands high and sturdy was posted.

Well-educated and experienced George W. Thompson retired as Judge of the Circuit Court in 1861. Along with other prominent men of Wheeling, he was arrested during the war for refusing to sign the Oath of Allegiance to the United States. Although opposing the secession of Virginia from the Union, he feared that the proposed formation of a new state would prove to be illegal. *(History and Government of West Virginia, by Virgil Lewis, 1896)*

By Bekah Karelis

According to the *Daily Intelligencer*, the Fourth of July was celebrated in Wheeling in 1862 as never before in the history of the city. "The businesses were all closed, and the whole population turned its attention to being patriotic. The city looked as if it was wrapped in millions of star spangled banners and little American flags. According to the program the bells of the city rung at an early hour in the morning, the cannon boomed from all quarters, waking the echoes and the people and bringing the world hereabouts to a sudden sense of its duty on the great and glorious occasion." The cannon that was "booming from all quarters" was a spoil of war. Captured by Gen. Benjamin Kelley at Romney, it was sent to Wheeling posthaste in order to aid in the celebrations.

A Soldier's Aid Society was organized in Wheeling with Governor Francis Pierpont on the Board of Directors. The society beseeched locals to help their cause. "Let us then do our part – let all, old and young, male and female, unite in this work of grateful love. Other states and cities are awake to this object and are sending contributions to their relief – still much more is needed and shall we be behind all the others?"

Fifty sick soldiers arrived in Wheeling on July 11 and were housed in the Sprigg House Hospital, bringing the total sick and wounded men to 166 in that hospital alone.

For those soldiers who were more intent to forget themselves and the role they played in the national conflict, a "gentle" reminder was sent out from Camp Carlile on July 21, 1862. "Notice is hereby given to all persons wearing the insignia of officers or soldiers of the United States Army and not entitled to do so, to immediately remove the same, else they will be publicly stripped of them and placed under arrest. All soldiers absent 'furlough' or otherwise, are again ordered to report immediately to avoid arrest as deserters."

Things were generally quiet in Wheeling, but the fate of the proposed new state was brought up several times at the U.S. Senate meetings in Washington. Senator Waitman T. Willey moved to take up the West Virginia statehood bill on both July 1 and July 7, and finally, on July 14, 1862, the issue came to the table for some serious debate.

Throughout the summer of 1862, when the Senate began considering admission of West Virginia to the Union, the debate on how to make West Virginia a "Free state" was entwined with the issue of statehood itself.

On July 1, 1862, senators debated a provision in West Virginia's proposed statehood bill that would free all children born of slaves after July 3, 1863. Restored Government of Virginia Sen. Waitman T. Willey pushed for gradual emancipation. Sen. Benjamin Wade of Ohio thought to free all slaves at a certain age, while Sen. Charles Sumner of Massachusetts argued for the immediate emancipation of all slaves.

Restored Government of Virginia Sen. John S. Carlile, a strong proponent of statehood up to this point, took a controversial stance. He wanted a statewide election on the issue of slavery instead of the proposed gradual emancipation amendment. Given the Confederate sympathies in several counties of western Virginia, this very well could have stalled statehood, irrevocably. His stance was unexpected and created animosity and some confusion among those who had been working with Carlile in the Senate on the statehood issue. These early debates continued to end without consensus.

The newspaper told of the exchanges between Sen. Wade and Carlile after Carlile spoke out against the statehood bill, "We notice in the debates on the new State in the U.S. Senate, on Monday, that Mr. Wade became very indignant at the course of Mr. Carlile, and openly charged him with endeavoring to defeat the new state, while pretending to be its friend."

Wade's exact words in the Senate debate were as follows. "He has gone back of their appointment; he has not only undertaken to find fault with what they have done, but he has undertaken to say that they were not really organized to do anything; and it is the first I have heard of any such thing. We have sat in committee with that gentleman; we have heard his arguments and illustrations on this subject; we have had many men of the proposed State before us, in council with us upon it; and here for the first time to-day we hear that the convention who framed this constitution really did not represent the people whom they professed to represent!"

A few weeks after Carlile's divisive vote, he gave a speech at the Athenaeum in Wheeling. The theater was crowded with spectators. He treated the subject of statehood lightly, telling the crowd that the "abolition appendages" to the statehood bill were his reason for voting against it. His umbrage was with the bill as the Senate amended it, not the bill that the Wheeling Convention created. The *Intelligencer* negated this stance, using Carlile's arguments in Senate against him " ... by proceeding to show that the Convention that formed it was a mere bogus Convention, the members of which represented scarcely any constituents, and whose constitution received only 19,000 of 47,000 votes. It was a blow at the whole new State project – by trying to show that there was no new State feeling among our people, and that the whole thing was unworthy of the attention of the Senate."

Carlile's vote against West Virginia statehood made him a traitor in the eyes of all who worked with him. He served the remainder of his term in the U.S. Senate until March 3, 1865, and was never again elected to political office.

Ultimately, the amendment written by the Restored Government of Virginia's Sen. Waitman T. Willey, which required only that the gradual emancipation clause be approved by a constitutional convention and not by a statewide election, was attached to the bill. That amendment would be known as the "Willey Amendment."

On July 14, 1862, the U.S. Senate approved the statehood bill with a vote of 23-17.

Historians may puzzle over the actions of John Carlile. Although one of the early proponents of statehood, as one of the initial West Virginia representatives in the U.S. Senate, he voted against it, insisting that a statewide election should be held on the issue of slavery within the borders of the proposed new state. He was subsequently viewed as a traitor and was never again elected to public office. *(Library of Congress)*

August 1862
By Ed Phillips

The Wheeling *Daily Intelligencer* reported on August 12, 1862, that John Carlin was recruiting in the city for the formation of an artillery battery. The first day brought 37 recruits, and by August 16th, 106 had joined. The unit was sworn into government service at Camp Carlile on August 20, 1862, as Battery D, First Virginia (Union) Light Artillery, also known locally as Carlin's Wheeling Battery. The battery received their guns and horses on September 9th and was then fully equipped and ready for service. On September 20, while returning to Wheeling Island after being downtown firing a salute, a beautiful black horse of one of the teams dropped dead – not a good beginning.

The unit was sent to Parkersburg for a few weeks, then on to Clarksburg and Beverly where they came under the command of General Robert Milroy. C. H. Sweeney reported that during the march from Beverly towards Winchester the unit picked up a goose and put it into a Silbey stove. The goose started to squawk, but Captain Carlin located it, and the goose immediately lost its head.

While in Buckhannon, the battery's minstrels, some ten in number, along with the battery's band, performed a show with much success. General Milroy was in attendance, along with many "shoulder straps" (officers) and ladies. The general was said to have enjoyed the performance so much that he honored the battery by having them put on an artillery performance firing at a target. He stated later that he had only once before witnessed such accuracy and that was during the late Mexican War by the Washington Battery. He was reminded that Captain Carlin was the top gunner in that battery – high praise for the Wheeling boys.

The unit was at the battle of First Winchester on June 14, 1863, when General Milroy's command was attacked. He ordered the city to be abandoned, leaving behind all baggage and artillery pieces. One man, Allen Stevens, was wounded. (The following year he was captured. After his release in 1865 he drowned in the *Sultana* disaster.) About 50 others were captured, but all were exchanged and back on duty in 23 days. While prisoners, they reportedly met several old friends who were serving in the Confederate army.

The remainder of the battery returned to Wheeling to recruit and refit. In late July 1863 Confederate General John Hunt Morgan attempted to cross the Ohio River into Virginia. One section of the battery (two guns) was sent down river to Captina, and the remainder remained stationed on Wheeling Island. Fearing the approach of Morgan, the state legislature decided to head up river from Wheeling toward the safety of Steubenville. Captain Carlin and one section of the battery loaded up a barge and accompanied them. Fortunately Morgan surrendered before he could reach the immediate area.

A large festival was held on the return of the battery to Wheeling, and money was raised for new instruments for their band. When the battery mustered out in 1865, the instruments were given to Mr. John Wallace, the band's director, to start a new band and music school.

In February 1864 part of the battery was sent to Greenland Gap, where they were said to have spent several weeks trout fishing. By April the unit was shipped up the Shenandoah Valley and came under the command of General Franz Sigel. On May 15th they were placed on the right of the line by Captain Carlin during the battle of New Market. It was a short but fierce fight during which three men were killed and five wounded. The battery also lost three guns when horses were killed and there was no way to remove the guns from the field. New Market was the worst day of the war for the Wheeling boys.

After the battle, the battery marched to Cedar Creek, where it was refitted and rested. About June 1st they again moved back up the valley, this time under the command of General David Hunter. On June 5th they were involved in a small engagement at Piedmont where the only member wounded was Jacob Honecker, who lost his right arm. The battery went on to Lexington after VMI was burned and began the retreat back down the valley. They came under fire at Salem and were attacked by 150 to 200 Confederate cavalry at Mason's Cove. Since the men were not armed, they scattered, with many being taken prisoner. All the guns and equipment were captured, with two guns taken and the rest burned. It was a sorry sight along the road for the rest of the army to march past.

The battery returned again to Wheeling to be refitted and equipped and then was sent to Fort Boreman in Parkersburg, where they remained until early February 1865. While there, the battery band came back to Wheeling several times to perform. Later in the month they were ordered to Clarksburg, where they remained until June 15th. When hearing of the surrender of General Robert E. Lee, some of the men of the unit found a barrel of ale in front of a bakery shop and took it to their camp, where it quickly disappeared. Captain Carlin ordered Corporal William Phillips to find the barrel, although he apparently knew that if anyone in the battery could fail to find it, it would be Phillips. Back in Wheeling the unit was discharged.

One other member of the battery should be mentioned – old dog Joe. He followed the battery from Winchester throughout the remainder of the war. He kept out of sight during the battles, showing that he had good sense. After discharge, Al Redman took Joe, but he didn't last long. Apparently peace didn't suit him.

When organized, the battery had 152 members, but with later recruits and replacements, 212 men served in it during the war. The unit had seven men killed or who died of wounds, eight wounded, nine who died in prison camps, three who deserted, and three who died in the *Sultana* disaster.

Irish immigrant John Carlin served with distinction in the Mexican-American War before organizing a Civil War artillery unit – nicknamed "Carlin's Battery." After the war, he worked as an accountant and then as Collector of Internal Revenue for the district. His gravesite in Greenwood Cemetery is often graced with a Union flag. *(Photo by Jeanne Finstein)*

By Margaret Brennan

September 1862 was a crucial month in the Civil War, with events ranging from an attempted robbery at the Custom House in Wheeling to the battles of Harpers Ferry, South Mountain, and Antietam, and Lincoln's proclamation of emancipation.

Early on, Camp Carlile, the troop training camp on Wheeling Island, held 2,000 men. One group, the 12th (Union) Virginia Regiment marched from the island to the B&O depot. "Their appearance created great sensation. The people flocked after them," the *Daily Intelligencer* reported. This sight was repeated many times through the month, with the troops often pausing at the *Intelligencer* office on Main Street and giving a cheer. The paper frequently sent copies to the soldiers at the camp.

News of the August 30 battle of Second Manassas/Bull Run was filtering in. "Our loss has been immense in government stores and in killed, wounded, and missing," the *Daily Intelligencer* reported.

The Wheeling Soldiers Aid Society, well known for its generosity under Jacob Hornbrook and Mr. Gilchrist, sent boxes of supplies to the sick and wounded at Martinsburg and Alexandria.

It was reported that two sisters, Mary and Elizabeth Peck of Moundsville, were jailed at the Athenaeum for refusing to take the oath of allegiance. James Bumgardner of Wheeling was arrested and jailed for using treasonable language. This happened quite often. "Rebel sympathizers will no longer be dallied with. They must take the oath or go to jail and stay there."

Gov. Francis Pierpont was in Washington and telegraphed for ten nurses to go to D.C. Eleven people promptly responded, including Alexander Laughlin and Mrs. Lydia Holliday. The governor felt the rebels were at the end of their rope.

Meanwhile, a Confederate force had captured Buckhannon, taking a lot of supplies. It was also reported that 20 Wheeling ambulances were shipped to D.C. And it seemed the government could not stop the sale of liquor to soldiers, who used ingenious ways to get off the island.

On Friday, September 5, a lengthy article described the Wednesday night attempt to rob the Custom House of $1,250,000. Fortunately, the burglars could not get the money out of the well-constructed vault. The newspaper took the army security to task, and the army responded in kind.

The paper also reported the presentation of a fine sword to Capt. John Carlin of the Wheeling Battery by his men. "The battery is composed of the best young men (150) in the city, and a deep interest will always be felt in its movements."

On September 6, a man wrote asking for help for the western Virginia sick and wounded. "Alexandria and Washington are nothing but vast hospitals." Col. Joseph Thoburn was reported ill of typhoid in Alexandria, and Jacob Hornbrook went to visit the hospitals there.

In military matters, Maj. Gen. Jesse Reno was put in command of the 3rd Army Corps. Gov. Pierpont asked that the people of western Virginia organize themselves for the protection of their communities. Lee's army had crossed the Potomac into Maryland on September 4, and by September 11 was active in the Hagerstown area. On September 14, Lee's forces engaged part of the Union army at the Battle of South Mountain, where it was reported "we have to lament the death of the gallant General Reno," born in Wheeling. Meanwhile, Gen. Thomas "Stonewall" Jackson had taken Harpers Ferry, capturing almost 12,700 soldiers, the most ever surrendered during the Civil War.

On Wednesday, September 17, the two armies collided at the Battle of Sharpsburg/Antietam, setting up the bloodiest day of the war. Approximately 23,000 soldiers were killed or wounded.

The medical corps faced a daunting challenge, and Clara Barton herself came to the battlefield with supplies and succor. This was the first great battle where the chief medical officer, Dr. Jonathan Letterman, who had served in Wheeling with Gen. William Rosecrans, put into effect his plan for triage and evacuation. A total of 200 ambulances had been sent from D.C., including many made in Wheeling, and the wounded were efficiently removed from the battlefield, instead of lying for days and dying.

The Confederate armies were generally on the move. The rebels, under Col. John McCausland and Col. William Loring, drove Col. Joseph Lightburn out of the Kanawha Valley, capturing the important salt works. Even the President was shot at as he traveled to his Soldiers and Sailors Home cottage. Mrs. Lincoln put her foot down, and he was then provided a suitable escort.

As the horror of Antietam sank in, a call was put out for relief supplies and surgeons. Gen. George McClellan telegraphed, "We may safely claim a victory." The Confederates began to retreat to Virginia and were engaged on September 19 at Shepherdstown, the largest battle fought on western Virginia soil.

On Wednesday, September 24, the *Daily Intelligencer* was filled with a momentous story. On September 22, Lincoln had announced that he would officially issue the Emancipation Proclamation on January 1, 1863, and the entire text was printed. It had become clear in the previous months that preserving the Union and dealing with slavery could not be separated. Many, including Frederick Douglass, had urged the President to speak to the issue. Finally, Lincoln resolved to take action and discussed the proclamation with his cabinet. They cautioned him to wait for a Union victory to announce his decision. Now the President had Antietam, so five days later he made his move.

The *Daily Intelligencer* applauded Lincoln's effort. "We say a thousand Amens to the proclamation." On September 25, the paper stated, "Slavery is the cause of this war. Had we not had slavery among us we would not have had this war. The President recognizes this great truth and so does the country."

On Saturday, September 27, a crowd went to the White House to serenade the President. In greeting them, he commented on the proclamation: "I can only trust in God I have made no mistake."

Successful businessman Jacob Hornbrook became known as the "soldiers' friend," due to his efforts to provide Wheeling soldiers with goods from home and for bringing their paychecks back to Wheeling to support their families. His son Henry served in the Union army under General Benjamin Kelley, and his daughter India married Kelley's son John. *(West Virginia Independence Hall Foundation)*

October 1862

By Robert DeFrancis

As West Virginia historians seek to commemorate events surrounding the 150th anniversary of the American Civil War, it seems fitting to cite the role played in the Northern Panhandle by the forerunners of two institutions of higher learning that continue to thrive.

During October of 1862, while the faculty of South Carolina College in Columbia was meeting to acknowledge that their institution had to be closed because of the Civil War, joining several other vacated colleges in the south, to the north both the West Liberty Academy and Bethany College, though pummeled by the war, remained open.

In an article written by Michael David Cohen in *The New York Times* earlier in the month, the plight of those southern colleges was detailed. History professor Cohen pointed out the South Carolina faculty members recorded in their minutes of that October 6 meeting that, "'the Confederacy had converted the school into a military hospital.' The students were all gone and no classes would meet again for several years."

Cohen said colleges were commandeered for use as hospitals or barracks by both the Confederate and Union armies as more and more young men left them to become soldiers. The experience for West Liberty Academy, now West Liberty University, and Bethany College was far different. West Liberty Academy was opened in 1837 and WLU celebrated its 175th anniversary in 2012. Bethany College opened three years later, in 1840, and is the oldest private college in the state.

In his book *West Liberty State College, The First 125 Years*, author Frank T. Reuter explained, "Chartered by the Legislature of Virginia on March 30, 1837, the Academy came about primarily through the efforts of the Reverend Nathan Shotwell," a Presbyterian preacher-educator. "West Liberty Academy was opened in 1838 with the Rev. Mr. Shotwell as principal. He and his wife were the only faculty members. Until a suitable school building could be built, the Shotwells began teaching in the main room of their home."

That first enrollment numbered 65 students, but Reuter said he could find no record on class make-up. Both boys and girls were admitted to the Academy but were strictly segregated, and "rigid regulations" prevented any meetings of the genders. These rules stayed in effect until 1904, he said. Immediately prior to the Civil War, Reuter said "students came to the Academy from a much larger area and in larger numbers" than previously, with a few students traveling all the way from Mississippi and Louisiana.

"Enthusiasm for war was quite strong in West Liberty," Reuter wrote. "Most of this enthusiasm was for the Union's cause, although its neighbor further north, Bethany, was strongly influenced by pro-Southern sympathies. Several companies of volunteers from the West Liberty district, including many Academy students, joined the Union Army."

The Academy's principal, as of 1857, was Professor A.F. Ross. As students joined the army, Reuter reported, Ross resigned in 1861 to devote himself to politics, trying to prevent Virginia from seceding from the Union. He became a prominent figure in the fight to form a new state and ultimately was elected to the Constitutional Convention and later to the first West Virginia State Legislature.

In relating West Liberty's service to the Union cause, Reuter's book cited "one of its most prominent citizens, and probably the most famous, was William Baker Curtis, who recruited a home guard from the Academy students when the war broke out. He drilled his company on the Bethany Pike and prepared them for any military eventuality." Curtis was commissioned a captain of the volunteer company he raised, and it ultimately was mustered into the Union Army as Company D, Twelfth West Virginia Volunteers.

"Curtis became a hero during the war and advanced rapidly in rank. Under his leadership, his brigade, after hard fighting, captured Fort Gregg at Petersburg in April 1865. He was rewarded with the rank of brigadier general." Curtis' son, J. Montgomery Curtis, 17, was commissioned a lieutenant in the Union Army and eventually was awarded a Medal of Honor for heroism.

"Education at West Liberty Academy continued despite the loss of principal, financial backers, and a large part of the student body," Reuter wrote. After the war, he said, "Mounting debt was destroying West Liberty Academy. The trustees decided the best solution was to attempt to sell the Academy building to the newly formed state of West Virginia for incorporation into the new educational system."

The purchase price was $6,000, and thus West Liberty Academy became "one of the first three institutions taken over by the new state. In the same month, February 1867, existing institutions at Morgantown and Huntington were purchased; these are now West Virginia University and Marshall University."

The Civil War experience of West Liberty Academy's neighbor, Bethany College, was related expertly by Dr. D. Duane Cummins, Bethany's president from 1988-2002, who spoke at the March 1, 2012 Founder's Day Convocation. According to Bethany's website reporting of the speech, "Cummins related his theme to the nation's present acknowledgment of the 150th anniversary of the Civil War and the event's relationship with the unique history and strong spirit of the college."

Cummins pointed out a bit of tragic Civil War foreshadowing. "In the fall of 1842, a tall, lean figure strolled across the campus at Bethany College. His name was Jefferson Davis." The speaker explained that Davis had arrived at Bethany to enroll his nephew, 17-year-old William Stamps from Mississippi. During his stay, Davis resided in the guest wing of Bethany College founder Alexander Campbell's home. "Six months later, Stamps ice skated on Buffalo Creek, where he fell and struck his head. That evening, suffering a seizure, he died."

Discussing the state of Virginia's vote on the issue of secession, Cummins said, "In all of Brooke County, only 109 votes supported secession. But 52 of those votes were in Bethany." He said many of those voting for secession were among Alexander Campbell's family, which also included directors of the Underground Railroad and a number of abolitionists.

"When the vote of Bethany residents was published in the Wellsburg paper, the little village of Bethany was labeled a 'nest' of secession," Cummins noted. During 1861, Cummins continued, "students in large number began to leave Bethany. Some went home, while most enlisted in the army. The student body was reduced to 38 and the faculty to two. Only five degrees were conferred in 1862, and enrollment soon fell again to 33." Across Brooke County, Cummins said, hatred steepened.

"In 1863, on July 3, commencement was held for four graduates. Only 10 trustees had been able to make the trip. Common sense suggested they should simply close the doors of the college," Cummins said. "But on that July third, the trustees, with no other asset than the ideal of Bethany College, made a fateful decision. And it is recorded in the minutes and the vote was unanimous that 'The operation of the college will continue in all respects.'" Enrollment that fall jumped 40 percent.

Cummins concluded, "It is the force of the Bethany ideal that carried the college through the Civil War. And it was never expressed more eloquently than by a Bethany student who lived through the epic just described and who later wrote, 'If my heart were opened, Bethany would be found written in its center.'"

Of interest also, concerning Bethany's Underground Railroad connection, is this information related to historic Bethany College structures found on a website for independent colleges. "Pendleton Heights, built between September 1, 1841, and June 20, 1842, was the home of William Kimbrough Pendleton. It is the oldest building on the Bethany College campus. During the Civil War, the Pendleton home was a station on the Underground Railway. Escaping slaves were hidden in the basement. Marcie Bright Banks of Pittsburgh recalls that her great grandmother's brother used to drive his hay wagon over to Bethany from Pennsylvania at night, hide the slaves under the hay, and then take them back to his home, where he hid them until it was safe to move them to West Middletown, Pa., where Alexander Campbell's sister, Jane Campbell McKeever, and her husband, Matthew McKeever, conducted Pleasant Hill Seminary, a seminary for young girls. Matthew McKeever hid the slaves in a loft, keeping this a secret from his family."

West Liberty's William Baker Curtis recruited a home guard from the Academy students when the war broke out, forming Company D, Twelfth West Virginia Volunteers. His son, J. Montgomery Curtis served as a lieutenant in the Union Army and was awarded a Medal of Honor for heroism. *(West Liberty University Archives)*

November 1862
By Joseph Laker

There were lots of skirmishes by both Union and Confederate forces during November 1862, but no major battles. Both sides were recovering from the bruising and frustrating battles of Antietam, Maryland, and Perryville, Kentucky. In the North, important political developments were taking place. The Senate passed legislation in July approving the creation of the state of West Virginia, but the House of Representatives voted to delay taking up the measure until December 10. On September 22nd President Lincoln issued a proclamation freeing all slaves in the areas of rebellion.

Wheeling was prosperous and trade was brisk in November 1862. New businesses were opening like George Story's Phoenix Ale Brewery. Key consumer goods could be purchased at the following prices: potatoes at 20¢ a peck, carrots 5¢ a bunch, beans 20¢ a peck, eggs 15¢ a dozen, and a live chicken 10¢. But, prices were beginning to rise, and workers were demanding higher wages. At the end of November, coal miners, who were receiving $2.50 per 100 bushel of coal mined, were demanding $3.00. Cart drivers who transported the coal, wanted $8.00 a week instead of $7.00. Mine owners, mainly bankers in Wheeling, refused the wage increases, but eventually were forced to give raises.

For entertainment citizens could watch one of the 11 military companies of the 4th Infantry Regiment of Virginia (Union) carry out frequent drills and marches at the Armory and Courthouse. Several major banquets were held at Washington Hall to honor the 1st Infantry Regiment of Virginia (Union) where military promotions were awarded. Newspapers reminded Wheeling citizens of unpleasant aspects of war such as rebel prisoners being escorted through town to the Athenaeum prison, the militia arresting supposedly pro-southern citizens for mocking the patrol, and soldiers shooting into the Ohio River from their camp on the island. The *Intelligencer* twice that month carried information about soldiers who were AWOL from their units and requested that citizens help in locating the individuals.

The issues most frequently mentioned in the press and on people's minds during November were Lincoln's proclamation emancipating slaves, the battle between the pro-Union *Intelligencer* and the pro-Southern *Wheeling Press*, and the struggle between the supporters of Senator Waitman Willey and those of Senator John Carlile.

After Lincoln released the proclamation emancipating the slaves in those areas of the country in rebellion, there was intense discussion about the proclamation. For many of the Union soldiers the goals of the war were widened beyond just preserving national unity to making the conflict a moral crusade to defend the freedom and equality of man. The *Intelligencer* ran stories that had been published throughout the nation defending Lincoln and condemning slavery.

Throughout the Civil War there was a vigorous battle between newspapers in Wheeling. The *Intelligencer*, founded in 1852 and edited by Archibald Campbell from 1856 to 1868, vigorously supported the Republican Party, the Lincoln presidency, the Union cause, and the attack on slavery. In almost every issue during November, Campbell found opportunities to attack the editors of rival papers, who answered back with their own nasty articles. Philip Moore, editor of the *Wheeling Union*, favored the Democratic Party, criticized Lincoln's policies, and supported Virginia's secession from the Union. Moore fled to the Confederacy on May 27, 1861 when public hostility to his position became too intense in Wheeling. The *Union* was renamed the *Wheeling Press*. Edited by Henry Moore, Philip's father, the *Press* adopted basically the same editorial policy of the *Union*, but with a more moderate tone. In November 1862, Moore's paper strongly supported Senator Carlile's position on statehood for West Virginia. Moore faced hostility from both the government and citizenry and the paper closed, only to be replaced by the Wheeling *Daily Register*, which adopted his editorial line.

The most contentious issue covered by Wheeling's newspapers was whether West Virginia would be accepted into the Union as a separate state from Virginia. The issue divided the political leadership of the Restored Government of Virginia, headed by Governor Francis Pierpont. The government was represented by its two Senators in Washington, D. C., John Carlile and Waitman Willey. Both men were successful lawyers who served as delegates to the Virginia Constitutional Convention of 1851-52. They opposed Virginia's secession from the Union and helped organize and participate in both Wheeling Conventions that created the Restored Government of Virginia (loyal to the Union) and created the movement for a separate state. Carlile demanded that statehood be approved by a vote by the people of those counties that would be included in the new state. Most supporters of the separate state movement like Waitman Willey thought that Carlile's referendum demand was misguided and an effort to delay and sabotage the effort to create a separate state. Willey offered a bill that required only the approval of a Constitutional Convention, the approach that was eventually adopted. Carlile continued to serve in the U. S. Senate until 1865 representing the Restored Government of Virginia, but Willey resigned from that position and was chosen as one of the first Senators to represent West Virginia. He served from 1863 to 1871.

By the end of November the Union forces were ready for a new military effort against the south, but these efforts in early December were not successful. Fighting would continue for two and one-half more years. But, for West Virginians December proved to be decisive. On December 10, the U. S. House of Representatives approved the legislation creating West Virginia as a new state and sent the bill to President Lincoln. Governor Pierpont, Senator Willey, and others lobbied the President. Lincoln approved the legislation on New Year's Eve provided that West Virginia modify its Constitution to bring an end to slavery. West Virginians made the necessary changes, and on April 20, 1863 Lincoln announced that West Virginia would begin its existence on June 20.

WHEELING, W. VA. SHOWING THE SUSPENSION BRIDGE AND THE EMBARKATION OF THE GERMAN RIFLES. Sketched by J. A. Fars

The Wheeling wharf was a very active place during the war, with military units being transported by riverboat to points south. This image shows the embarkation of the German Rifles. *(Ohio County Public Library Archives)*

December 1862
By Kate Quinn

Early in December of 1862, the *Daily Intelligencer* carried an editorial saying, "Glory to God in the highest, West Virginia has been admitted to the Union. The 35th state has been added to the Constitution. All your sacrifices, all your devotions, all your patience and suffering is at last gloriously repaid. People of Wheeling, you who have gained so much by this success, shall we not have such a demonstration here as will be worthy of our ancient name and fame? Throw out your banners this morning. Tonight we suggest let the people assemble at some place suitable where there will be room enough to hear some of the numerous excellent speakers who are in the city and will be present."

But there was not much in the way of a celebration in the city, though in Moundsville a 35-gun salute was fired "in honor of this glorious result. We are free, we are free! Glorious news!" they shouted. By a vote of 96 to 55, West Virginia had become an independent state.

Although the city of Clarksburg had a huge celebration, Wheeling was busy preparing for Christmas and probably its citizens decided to wait until June for their commemoration. Though, the newspaper did comment that, "Our people are out in crowds congratulating each other on being free from the shackles that for so many years held them fast."

The New York Times commented on our statehood and called the boundaries of our new state "a miracle of crookedness."

Wheeling's people enjoyed "the biting cold air, cold feet, delightful winter sleigh ride parties with the accessories of huge buffalo robes, ringing sleigh bells, foaming steeds, and above all, pretty girls."

In the middle of December, the Battle of Fredericksburg occurred with heavy losses on the Union side. Union Gen. Ambrose Burnside did not receive his pontoon bridges in time to transport his forces across the Rappahannock River, so Generals Robert E. Lee and Thomas "Stonewall" Jackson prevailed. The plan to capture Richmond was stalled.

Meanwhile, the steamer *Boston* 2 brought 37 prisoners to Wheeling and turned them over to the provost marshal of the Athenaeum. Among these prisoners "was the somewhat famous female soldier, Harry Fitsalleu." An interview with the prisoner, who was dressed in a tight-fitting cavalry uniform, was held to determine if there was truth in the charge that he/she was a Southern spy. She said her name was Marian McKinsey, from Glasgow, Scotland. Her mother had died when she was an infant, and her father had brought her to this country when she was 4. Since her father had died shortly thereafter, she was left alone "to make her living in various ways." She educated herself and began a career on the stage, but found it not to her taste and so traveled and took various jobs.

After the war broke out, she enlisted in a Kentucky regiment at Newport and served two months. "Upon her sex being discovered, she had to quit. She enlisted several times after this in various regiments and was several times arrested." The last time she was arrested was in Charleston, in men's apparel. When told she would be detained until her statements could be corroborated, she said, "Very well, I cannot help it. I have violated the law in assuming men's apparel."

The day after Christmas, an editorial in the *Daily Intelligencer* read, "Christmas passed on without any occurrence sufficiently remarkable to require practical notice. The day was dark and cloudy reminding one very unpleasantly of the old saying that a 'green Christmas makes a fat churchyard.' There were several little spurts of rain during the day, and the sun never once appeared to brighten or heighten the jollities of the occasion. Services were held in most of the churches and most everybody appeared to have an engagement to dine out upon roast turkey, venison and cranberry jelley (sic).

"In the streets there was a great intermingling of small boys, Jackson crackers and torpedoes. Retail dealers in these explosives tell us that they never had such a demand upon them. From morning till night there was a continuous popping, fizzing, and blowing. Exploded fire crackers lay upon sidewalks as thick as the leaves that now rustle in the woods and the air was pregnant with 'villainous saltpeters.'

"We regret to say that a great many people forgot what was good for themselves and due to the community on the glorious occasion, and took in more ardent spirits than was consistent with good order and sobriety. The consequence was that there were more riotous proceedings, particularly during the night, than usual, though we heard of no serious brawls. The general impression among people of all ages was that Cris Kringle was a pretty good fellar, who only comes once a year and who is always welcome."

Undoubtedly many Wheeling families wished for Christmas furloughs for their loved ones. This image from *Harpers Weekly* shows the happiness of one such family. *(Harpers Weekly)*

By Seán P. Duffy

Abraham Lincoln signed two documents of interest to the people of Wheeling over the New Year's holiday of 1862-63. On New Year's Eve, he signed the West Virginia statehood bill, and less than twenty-four hours later on New Year's Day, he signed the final version of the Emancipation Proclamation. Despite the mythology attached to them over subsequent decades, at the time, both measures were viewed by the President as "expedient" means by which to advance the Union's war effort.

Introduced on September 22, 1862, after the Union "victory" at Antietam, the Preliminary Emancipation Proclamation promised that on January 1, 1863, "all persons held as slaves within any State or designated part of a State, the people whereof shall then be in rebellion against the United States, shall be then, henceforward, and forever free…"

The morning of the day in question found the President shaking hundreds of hands at a New Year's Day "levee." He worried aloud that if his signature on the final Emancipation Proclamation showed any signs of a trembling hand, people might conclude that he harbored "compunctions." He signed boldly, reportedly declaring, "I never in my life felt more certain that I was doing right, than I do in signing this paper."

But Lincoln knew it was not enough. In his popular film about the sixteenth president, Stephen Spielberg presents an Abraham Lincoln deeply concerned about the ratification of the Thirteenth Amendment abolishing slavery, because it "…settles the fate for all coming time, not only of the millions in bondage but of unborn millions to come…We must cure ourselves of slavery. This amendment is that cure." Spielberg's Lincoln clearly views the amendment as the curative, moral step untaken by his Emancipation Proclamation (merely "a fit and necessary war measure for suppressing [the] rebellion")—to link the end of slavery with the unfulfilled Founders' proposition that, "all men are created equal."

The Emancipation Proclamation was an unadorned step in an

expedient direction, and on January 3, 1863, the Wheeling *Daily Intelligencer* expressed its support. "True to the moral instincts of his nature, true to his solemn oath to preserve the Government, Abraham Lincoln has issued his proclamation...a very plain and easily understood document...momentous in its import and destined yet to be so conspicuous in everlasting history..."

Yet, what was to become the new state of West Virginia was specifically exempted. Emancipation would apply only in the states in rebellion, including, "Virginia, (except the forty-eight counties designated as West Virginia...and which excepted parts, are for the present, left precisely as if this proclamation were not issued.)" Despite Lincoln's signature on the statehood bill only hours before, the final admission of West Virginia would require a compromise on slavery known as the "Willey Amendment," which featured gradual emancipation. Of course, the 1865 ratification of the Thirteenth Amendment would render the entire issue moot.

Spotting a golden marketing opportunity, Wheeling merchants took full advantage of the attention paid to the emancipation saga. Augustus Pollack, for example, began running a regular advertisement under the heading, "Another Proclamation" in which he offered "at less than New York prices" hoop skirts, portfolios for the army, children's carriages, undershirts and drawers, among other items.

Like the Emancipation Proclamation, President Lincoln's decision to sign the West Virginia statehood bill was also motivated by expediency. Another military defeat at Fredericksburg convinced Lincoln of the timeliness of statehood, a move sure to weaken the Old Dominion while strengthening the Union.

On January 3, the pro-statehood *Intelligencer* thanked the president profusely for "Our Greatest New Year's Gift. New Year's Day was made truly and perpetually memorable to the people of West Virginia by the act of the President...signing their New State bill... People gathered in the streets and the word passed like electricity from mouth to mouth. In an hour, everybody seemed to know it and the streets beamed with joyous groups of people exchanging hearty and happy congratulations over the glorious event... The old cannon was again brought out...and again the hills and dells of our grand old river valley were made to wake the echoes that told the joy of a people made free...The president's name will henceforth be canonized by the people of West Virginia as the redeemer of their country and themselves...'God bless Abraham Lincoln!'"

Elsewhere in the city, New Year's Day passed with "a good deal of drunkenness – a fact attributable not so much to the quantity of the liquor consumed as to it execrable quality."

In contrast to Wheeling's celebratory mood, most of the nation would remember that New Year's holiday for the bloody Battle of Stones River (second Murfreesboro), where troops under General William Rosecrans held their ground against a Confederate assault led by General Braxton Bragg. More than three thousand men were killed, among them Henry Sharp, a Wheeling boy serving in the 2nd Ohio Regiment. An additional sixteen thousand men were wounded, among them Lt. Col. Frank Askew, a St. Clairsville resident serving in the 15th Ohio Regiment, who "distinguished himself by deeds of heroism and punished the enemy severely."

By January 8, "the first train from Baltimore over the Baltimore and Ohio railroad, since the last destruction by the rebels," arrived in Wheeling. "If Stonewall Jackson and his crowd will only manage to mind their own business," the *Intelligencer* observed, "the road will soon be in as good condition as ever."

By mid-month, Wheeling's weather turned foul with "three inches of slush upon the sidewalks, which soaked through the heaviest cowhide boots." A cold spell gripped the city, closing up "Wheeling Creek with ice" but affording "fine skating." Small boys "assembled in squads on the street...for the purpose of pelting pedestrians and sleighs with snowballs," while others engaged in "sledging" near Monroe Street. Meanwhile, "a couple of children of large growth supposed to be under the influence of some intoxicating fluid, borrowed a sled from a child of less mature years, and thought to take a sled ride." They knocked down several ladies and gentlemen and ended up "like Jack and Jill except that they did not go up the hill to draw a pail of water."

Despite the foul weather, Wheeling's legendary lawlessness continued unabated. The *Intelligencer* published a series of reports concerning a "ghastly and horrible ghost...perambulating around East Wheeling..." near the Hempfield Railroad depot. It wore a cowl and "heavy skins" presenting an "outré appearance." Armed ghost hunters began scouring the alleys in search of the phantom. The East Wheeling ghost created a sensation and spawned imitators. "There is scarcely a section of the city now but can boast of its ghost," the *Intelligencer* reported.

Gangs of "garrotters," who choked and robbed their victims, joined the apparitions in terrorizing the city. When one of them garroted a printer who worked for the *Intelligencer*, the editors could not resist observing that, "the individual must have been insane or drunk for certainly no sober person with anything like a decent supply of the commonest horse sense would attempt to rob a printer."

Later in January, the "notorious ruffian" John Brady of Wheeling was stabbed three times and killed by a man named Lockwood aboard the steamer *St. Patrick*. Brady had been "cutting, slashing and beating people about this city for a number of years," and was known along the rivers as a "wrecker and pirate...a very violent man, particularly when under the influence of liquor."

On a more positive note, Captain Downing established a horse hospital on Wheeling Island for "dilapidated and indigent horses," employing a revolutionary "hydropathic" system to rehabilitate the animals. Most reportedly emerged "like new horses," which did not escape the notice of Secretary of War Stanton, who authorized Captain Downing to rehabilitate all of the "superannuated horses in Western Virginia."

Despite Downing's success, the residents of Wheeling Island attempted to "secede" from the city. A petition signed by "nearly all of the property owners" on Wheeling Island was submitted to the House of Delegates to "exclude the Island from the limits of the city." The petitioners claimed they had to submit to "burdensome taxation" while being unable to "enjoy any of the benefit of city improvements (such as water, gas, etc.)."

Business remained brisk for Provost Marshal Major Joseph Darr at Wheeling's military prison, the Athenaeum. Thirty-three prisoners captured near Winchester arrived from Cumberland on January 3, and ten more from Braxton County on the 8th. Not long after "some three or four persons were arrested...and committed to the Athenaeum for yelling for Jeff Davis. The butternuts...permitted their zeal to outrun their discretion."

The notorious female prisoner, Harry Fitsalleu (Marion McKinsey), refused to wear women's clothing purchased for her by Major Darr, "but clings to the cavalry pea-jacket and pantaloons in which she soldiered through the Kanawha Valley. The reason assigned is that she is not provided with hoops." A second female prisoner, Mary Jane Green, who was jailed for cutting down federal telegraph wires and handling rebel mail, soon joined Fitsalleu. Both women were said to be "very rebellious." Seventeen-year-old cavalry soldier, Mary Jane Prater, joined the group on January 23. "In view of the late mutiny upon this account among the female prisoners," Major Darr prudently asked her if she would wear female clothing without hoops. She said she would "see how she looked first." Darr promptly sent her to the city jail for "safe keeping."

Ellen Brady, a pastry cook at the McLure House, was accused of "handling rebel mail matter...and suspicious conversation with prominent rebels who appear to be making a tool of her." She was arrested but released after taking the oath of allegiance.

Though their reaction was not noted in the January 1863

Intelligencer, Wheeling's African American community continued to celebrate "Emancipation Day" well into the twentieth century, usually on or near the anniversary of the September 22, 1862, preliminary proclamation. The 1896 observance was typical. After a parade of various black fraternal societies over the suspension bridge, the festivities took place at the State Fair grounds on the Island, and featured speeches by dignitaries, horse racing, bicycle racing, sack racing, wheelbarrow racing, and baseball games. An evening banquet and dance featuring the music of the opera house band was held at Turner's hall. Lincoln School principal J. McHenry Jones served as master of ceremonies.

On January 1, 1863, President Abraham Lincoln boldly signed the Emancipation Proclamation, worrying aloud that any trembling on his part might indicate his indecision. *(Library of Congress)*

By Wilkes Kinney

In July of 1862, Massachusetts Gov. John Andrews met with Francis Shaw, an avid abolitionist and a wealthy heir to a fortune, and a runaway slave named Frederick Douglass, who was a dazzling speaker with a baritone voice.

The group of men wanted to recruit a troop of black (colored) soldiers to fight in the Civil War. The governor petitioned the Secretary of War to sanction such a recruiting effort. Secretary of War Edwin M. Stanton did not sanction the recruiting until January 1863, the same month as the Emancipation Proclamation. The 54th Massachusetts was commissioned in March 1863.

The establishment of a regiment of black soldiers was not without problems. The first obstacle was who would be the person to lead this black regiment. Stanton believed it would be better if all black troops were under the supervision of white officers. Robert Gould Shaw, the son of prominent wealthy abolitionist Francis Shaw, was hand picked by Gov. Andrews and called upon to lead this unit. Shaw had the rank of captain but was promoted to the rank of colonel. Stanton also believed it would be better if the officers under Shaw were white. Andrews urged Norwood Penrose to be lieutenant colonel (second in command) before Stanton picked his men. Most of the officers, however, were from prominent Massachusetts families.

There were many obstacles in recruitment of black troops. Many in the Massachusetts black communities were free men and small business owners. They did not want to go out to fight, and they did not want their sons going out to fight for what many free blacks viewed as a white man's war.

However, with the help of Douglass and the enlistment of Douglass' son as one of the first recruits, the 54th soon reached its authorized strength of 1,100 men. The troops were free men, runaway slaves, educated men, and illiterate men. When the troop was not training or in drills, the illiterate members were taught to read and write.

Morale was low because most of the recruits were eager for battle, but they were initially used as a labor force and as scavengers of battlefields and captured farms. The unit was notified that if any of the soldiers were captured in battle, they would be put back into slavery, imprisoned, or hanged. Additionally, white officers were told they would be hanged for treason if caught leading troops against the Confederate states.

The unit remained hungry to fight. They did get the opportunity to fight at Grimball's Landing, Battle of Olustee, Battle of Honey Hill, Battle of Boykin Mill, and the second Battle of Fort Wagner. At the Battle of Olustee, Sgt. William H. Carney received the Medal of Honor, becoming the first African American to receive this honor during the Civil War. Today, some of Carney's family members reside in the Steubenville area. Shaw and 60 percent of the 54th Massachusetts soldiers were killed in the second battle of Fort Wagner.

Black soldiers first fought for the Union beginning in the spring of 1863. One of the most well known units was the 54th Massachusetts, led by Robert Gould Shaw. This photograph is of Sgt. Tom Strawn of Company B, 3rd U.S. Colored Troops, Heavy Artillery Regiment. *(Library of Congress)*

March 1863

By Joseph Laker

By March 1863 the war had lasted almost two years, and the people of both North and South were war weary and frustrated by the lack of any clear breakthrough. The stresses of war and domestic tragedies were evident in news stories of the day. Wheeling was troubled by burglaries, robberies, murders, fires, and the transport through the city of war prisoners and deserters who ended up at the Athenaeum prison in downtown Wheeling.

Military leaders of both North and South worked to rebuild their depleted armies after the fierce battles of December 1862 and to prepare for the battles to come. The Union navy tightened its blockade of southern ports and occupied coastal areas of the confederacy. No major battles occurred in the country during March, but numerous skirmishes did take place causing considerable loss of life and destruction of property.

On March 3, 1863, Congress passed a conscription bill. All males between the ages of 20 and 45 were liable for military service except for the unfit and those exempted. One could buy a substitute for $300, and more than 70% of men drafted did so. The law led to serious protests in northern states and riots in New York City, but it had little effect in northwestern Virginia where more than enough men volunteered to fill the quota. Commenting on those opposed to the draft, the *Intelligencer* sarcastically listed ways to avoid military service: go to Canada, go crazy, drink six gallons of whiskey, cut off your forefinger, or plunk down $300.

Business in Wheeling remained prosperous, but the Federal government's seizure of many of the steamboats on the river for the war effort hampered shipping and contributed to rising prices. Butter rose to 30-35 cents a pound, eggs to 18 to 20 cents a dozen, and potatoes at $1.00 a bushel. Two chickens cost 25 cents. Quoting letters received from Richmond, the *Intelligencer* claimed prices were much worse in the blockaded confederacy with butter in Richmond costing $2.75 a pound and cornmeal $5.00 a bushel.

The people of Wheeling were entertained late Friday morning,

March 13, when more than 1000 gathered on the hill above the city to observe the public hanging of Robert "Doc" Poole, convicted of the killing of Adam Buch, a Wheeling barkeep. A festive atmosphere prevailed as Poole said goodbye to fellow prisoners and was conveyed through the crowd in a cart to the place of execution. Hymns were sung, prayers recited, and Poole gave a brief speech urging people to renounce sin and love God. When asked by Sheriff Loring if he was ready, Poole answered "the quicker the better." After Poole had hung about an hour, he was declared dead by two physicians. While "Doc" Poole was dying in Wheeling, his younger brother, Alexander, was in a Parkersburg jail awaiting trial for the murder of a fellow soldier.

More wholesome entertainment was provided by an exhibition of J. Insco Williams' "Panorama of the Bible," a set of pictures depicting scenes of the Bible covering 4,000 square yards. The exhibition at Washington Hall from March 19 through the 31st could be viewed for 25 cents by adults and 15 cents by children. A 40-page book showing each biblical scene with scriptural explanatory text was available. A Cincinnati based artist, Williams was creating a 10,000 square foot panorama inspired by the Civil War at the time of the Bible exhibit.

When Lincoln and Congress approved of West Virginians' request to establish a new state in December 1862, they did so with the condition that the state constitution be amended to require the gradual emancipation of slaves. The Wheeling Convention reconvened, February 12-20, amended the Constitution, and asked the people to approve of the change by referendum on March 26. The Convention authorized the publication of an "Address of the Delegates to their Constituents" to acquaint the voters with the main objections to the Constitution and their refuting arguments. Ten thousand copies of the "Address" were distributed throughout western Virginia. Numerous meetings were held between the close of the Convention and voting day by both supporters and opponents. The *Intelligencer* strongly supported speakers favoring the Constitution, called New Staters, such as Senator Waitman Willey and Peter Van Winkle, while criticizing those opposed, like Senator John Carlile and the former democratic Congressman from Ohio County, Sherrard Clemens. Along the Ohio River the anti-New State proponents like Clemens frequently found their meetings and speeches disrupted, sometimes with violence by New Staters. The *Intelligencer* derisively branded New State opponents like Clemens as Copperheads (poisonous snakes) or butternuts (getting their name from Confederates who used dye from butternut, white walnut, to dye their homespun uniforms, usually a yellowish tan). In areas where pro-Southern sentiment was strong, New Staters faced similar sentiment. In Wheeling the *Intelligencer* constantly traded insults with Henry Moore's *Wheeling Press* during this month of campaigning, and the *Intelligencer* gloated over the closing of its rival on March 23rd.

When it became clear that the voters would approve the amended constitution, Carlile and Clemens urged their supporters to boycott the election claiming the vote could not be fair as there would be no secret ballots and intimidation would occur. Francis Pierpont, Governor of the Restored Government of Virginia, guaranteed that Union troops would ensure a free and fair election.

The official results of the March 26 referendum showed 28,321 voting in favor to 572 opposing the amended Constitution. Election officials threw out 422 affirmative votes as being improperly cast. The vote in Ohio County was 1806 yes to 8 no. Voting was very light in many eastern and southern counties, and no results came in from Calhoun, Logan, McDowell, Mercer, Pocahontas, Raleigh, Webster, or Wyoming counties. Nonetheless, after receiving the official election result, Lincoln announced that West Virginia would be recognized as the nation's thirty-fifth state on June 20, 1863. The pro-Union, New Staters had reason to celebrate.

New York rioters who opposed the draft burned the colored orphan asylum on the corner of Fifth Avenue and Forty-Sixth Street. Since Ohio County regularly met its quota of recruits, the draft was not an issue in Wheeling. *(Library of Congress)*

April 1863

By John Bowman

Union General Ambrose Burnside's Army of the Potomac, still staggering from its December defeat at Fredericksburg, began its ill-fated offensive against Lee's Army of Northern Virginia January 20, 1863. This disastrous campaign, known as the "Mud March" lasted only three days and resulted in Lincoln's removal of Burnside. On January 25th, Lincoln replaced Burnside with Major General Joseph "Fighting Joe" Hooker. Following the Battle of Fredericksburg, Wheeling's Shriver Grays, Company G, 27th Virginia Infantry, CSA, under the command of Captain Daniel Shriver, encamped in and around Winchester, Virginia. Both Lee and Hooker's armies settled into winter quarters in unrelenting rains and awaited the warmer days of spring.

Morale in the Union army was low; as many as 200 men per day were deserting. Hooker reported a total of 85,000 men and officers missing when he took command. The general made many leadership and tactical changes and persuaded Lincoln to issue a general proclamation of amnesty to all deserters who would rejoin their commands by April 1. He instituted a (morale building) badge system giving each division its own recognizable insignia. By April 1, 1863, under Hooker's leadership, the army's morale had been restored. The Army of the Potomac was a formidable force, well supplied and well-equipped numbering nearly 134,000 men. However morale on the home front had sunk to a new low. Say it or not, everyone was tiring of war. The North's first conscription act was implemented in March indicating to many that a long struggle was on the horizon.

On April 2, a "bread riot" took place in Richmond, which would be followed later in the month in Raleigh. Several hundred women marched on the Capitol, confronted Governor John Letcher, and demanded relief. A shortage of food and basics and hyperinflation was taking its toll. The armies, in order to feed the hungry troops, had stripped the Virginia countryside leaving little for the civilian population. Confederate President Jefferson Davis appeared on the scene and threw a hand-full of coins into the crowd. Many of the protesting women were later arrested, convicted, and imprisoned.

On April 3, Hooker's headquarters received a telegram announcing Lincoln's arrival scheduled for the next day. On April 4, President Lincoln gathered a small entourage including Mrs. Lincoln aboard the *Carrie Martin* and steamed down the Potomac to visit General Hooker, meet with him, and discuss Hooker's future war strategy.

On April 4, the *Intelligencer* reported that Jenkins Raider prisoners captured at Point Pleasant had arrived at Wheeling's Athenaeum prison. On April 12, 70 more Rebel prisoners arrived on the steamer *Eagle*. On April 14, three Confederate spies from Buckhannon were brought to the prison. April 20th saw the arrival of 37 prisoners, 2 deserters, and 2 women of whom one, Miss Jennie DeHart, was a rebel spy. The other woman, Elizabeth Hays, who went by the name of "Peg Leg," was described as a "bad egg."

On April 6, Lincoln reviewed the Army of the Potomac's First, Sixth, Eleventh, and Twelfth Army Corps, the Cavalry Corps, and the 1st West Virginia Light Artillery ("Wheeling's Finest"), and Battery D (Capt. John Carlin's "Wheeling Battery"). Two days later, he reviewed the remaining two-thirds of the Army of the Potomac; as many as 70,000 men passed in review that day.

April 12, 1863, marked the second anniversary of the war. The Civil War had started April 12, 1861 at 4:30 a.m., when Confederate batteries opened fire on Fort Sumter in Charleston Harbor. The *Intelligencer* picked up this article from the Springfield, Massachusetts Republican newspaper, "The Author of *Life in the Iron Mills*, Miss Harding has been spending some time in New York with the wife of Gen. J.C. Fremont. Miss Harding is a native of Virginia and there, during the General's brief campaign, 'Our Jessie' first met her."

The President, Secretary of War Edwin M. Stanton, and Major General Henry W. Halleck joined Hooker at Aquia on April 19 to further discuss strategy. None considered Virginia the most important theater of war at that time. Each thought General Ulysses S. Grant's Mississippi operations more important. At 10:30 p.m., April 16, seven ironclad gunboats, including the ironclad *Lafayette*, three transports, and one of Charles Ellet, Jr.'s rams, ran the Vicksburg Blockade, a most important accomplishment. The Wheeling *Intelligencer* reported in April that Wheeling's "Missouri Iron Works" was furnishing the iron plate used on the Federal ironclads.

Lincoln thought that when Grant could take Vicksburg, it would be the turning point of the war. Splitting the states of the Confederacy along the line of the Mississippi River, the heart of the celebrated "Anaconda Plan" would seal the fate of the Confederacy. Lincoln and Halleck saw General Rosecrans' movements as second in importance and judged Hooker's Virginia activities, third.

On April 20, Proclamation 100, admitting West Virginia into the Union, was made by President Lincoln. It read:

Whereas by the act of Congress approved the 31st day of December last the State of West Virginia was declared to be one of the United States of America, and was admitted into the Union on an equal footing with the original States in all respects whatever, upon the condition that certain changes should be duly made in the proposed constitution for that State; and Whereas proof of a compliance with that condition, as required by the second section of the act aforesaid has been submitted to me: [At Wheeling, April 16, the president of the West Virginia constitutional convention certified the vote on the amended constitution and submitted it to the President] Now, therefore, be it known that I, Abraham Lincoln, President of the United States, do hereby, in pursuance of the act of Congress aforesaid, declare and proclaim that the said act shall take effect and be in force from and after sixty days from the date hereof (June 20, 1863).

On April 26, a convention of the Union and New State men met and selected delegates for the upcoming May 6 Parkersburg Convention. Meanwhile, Governor Francis H. Pierpont was making plans for the Restored Government of the State of Virginia to move to Alexandria, Virginia.

On April 27, Gen. Hooker moved his army towards Chancellorsville. Lee would begin his move to Chancellorsville on May 1. The Wheeling Shriver Grays, serving under General Stonewall Jackson, would be part of the Chancellorsville campaign, joining the recently organized 36th Virginia Cavalry Battalion under the command of Major James Sweeney of Wheeling.

Near noon on April 30, General Ulysses S. Grant began landing Federal troops south of Vicksburg. The consensus was that the end was near.

Ironworks in Wheeling provided heavy plate to protect Union boats during the Civil War. Suspension Bridge designer Charles Ellet, Jr., was mortally wounded while serving on an ironclad ram boat in the Mississippi. Pictured here is the ironclad *USS Essex*. *(Library of Congress)*

By Kate Quinn

In the month of May 1863, Wheeling newspapers were full of the shocking news of the death of Gen. Thomas "Stonewall" Jackson at the Battle of Chancellorsville. Eight days after being shot accidentally by one of his own men, Jackson died of pneumonia, weakened by the shock of having his left arm amputated. Born in Clarksburg, the general earned his nickname "Stonewall" at the First Battle of Manassas, where other generals exclaimed that Jackson and his men stood like a stone wall in the face of Union forces. Others say he obtained the nickname because his men fought from behind a stone wall and won the day.

Jackson had attended West Point with George McClellan and others, then fought in the Mexican War and lost his hearing standing too near artillery. Returning from that war, he and his wife purchased a house in Lexington, home of Virginia Military Institute. This house later served as the county hospital. It is said that as a professor at VMI, Jackson memorized his lectures and if interrupted by a question would have to start from the beginning of his lesson.

T.M. Harris, a colonel in the 10th Virginia, wrote to the *Daily Intelligencer* from Webster in Taylor County stating that he had met and interviewed deserters from Jackson's brigade who claimed that "he would be shot by his own men, the first engagement they should get into." These men listed their grievances as being forced into service against their will; that they were treated worse than dogs; that Jackson was "the greatest old tyrant in the world;" that he did not regard the life of a man; that his troops were kept at half rations; that some were shot for desertion; and that they were tied up and whipped for being absent without leave.

Robert E. Lee held Jackson in his highest esteem and wrote to him after his injury, "You have lost your left arm and I, my right arm and my heart."

In Wheeling, meanwhile, all talk was of the Jones-Imboden raiders who the citizens feared would attack the city. Confederate cavalry Gen. William "Grumble" Jones and Gen. John D. Imboden had three goals in mind: disrupt the B&O railroad at Oakland, Maryland, and Grafton, cut telegraph lines, and weaken federal control of the area.

At Fairmont, the raiders threw Gov. Francis Pierpont's library into the street and burned it. In Morgantown, they captured horses and supplies. One of the raiders later returned to the town to become postmaster and later president of West Virginia University. At Burning Springs, Jones set fire to barrels of oil, which then set the Little Kanawha River on fire.

In all, the raid netted 700 prisoners, 1,000 cattle, and 1,200 horses, with 16 railway bridges burned plus one tunnel, two railway cars and several boats. Thankfully, the raid was short-lived, and Wheeling was never in any real danger.

In other news, there was speculation of a war with England over the English propensity to build and supply war ships to the Confederacy. "A day of reckoning" was threatened, and many felt we had "an account to be settled."

As relief from the trials of war, Wheeling anxiously awaited the Robinson Circus, which featured Arabian horses, ostriches, "the horned horse," "the last of his race," and a splendid performing zebra. Master James Robinson had "just returned from abroad, the Prince Equestrian in the world" who was described as "the naked horse champion – in all his wonderful achievements." It was not stated whether it was Master James or the horse that was naked. The circus proudly touted a "huge waterproof firmament," 170 men and horses, and "two great clowns."

A plague of 17-year locusts infested the city, and citizens were told that, "locusts do not eat during migration."

Also in the news were Gov. Pierpont's plans to go to eastern Virginia to set up a capital.

At Parkersburg, Arthur Boreman was elected governor of the new state of West Virginia, while Pierpont continued as governor of the

Restored Government of Virginia, living above his office in Alexandria.

Mysteriously, there was no mention in the May newspapers of plans for a day of celebration of our statehood on June 20.

Thomas J. "Stonewall" Jackson was probably the second most well known Confederate commander, behind only Robert E. Lee. Many considered him the most gifted tactical commander in U.S. history. His death was a severe setback to the Confederacy. *(Library of Congress)*

June 1863
By David Javersak

In the 1960s, the definitive textbook history of the United States in the mid Nineteenth Century—James Randall and David Donald's *The Civil War and Reconstruction*—described statehood for West Virginia as "an offspring of a species of legal fiction." Other writers have been less kind, branding the state's creation as unconstitutional and illegal. West Virginia's Archives and History web site contains an expansive account of statehood and key primary documents. It is provocatively entitled: "A State of Convenience."

The locus of this fictitious species, this illegality of history, this work of convenience was Wheeling, in 1860, the state's largest city west of the Blue Ridge, the fourth largest in Virginia, and the 63rd most populous city in the United States. Here, in 1861, 1862, and 1863, western Virginians stood strong against dismemberment of the Union, pushed a series of actions which re-organized Virginia's government, crafted a new constitution, and created a new state.

The delegates to the Wheeling Conventions succeeded in creating the 35th star in the American Flag, and most citizens then and now believe the major reasons for Virginia's division were unresolved sectional differences, notably slavery, education, internal improvements, and equitable representation in the Virginia Legislature. But sectional differences existed in other states, and these did not lead to dismemberment. Moreover, the actions taken at these conventions did not represent the will of the majority of the state's residents.

Beginning with South Carolina, Deep South states began to secede a month after President Lincoln's election in November 1860. By the time Virginia held its Secession Convention in February 1861, eight states had already joined the Confederate States of America. The Virginia delegates did not take a vote until April 4, when they voted 85 to 45 against secession. Eight days later, Confederates bombarded Fort Sumter, and Lincoln's call for troops to suppress this rebellion emboldened Virginia secessionists who pushed through the Ordinance of Secession by a vote of 88 to 55 on April 17, a stark reversal of the earlier vote. This ordinance required voter ratification at the spring election on May 23.

The vast majority of the 55 no votes came from counties in modern-day West Virginia, especially from the counties bordering the Ohio River and in close proximity to Pennsylvania. Nevertheless, delegates from Wetzel, Ritchie, Pleasants, and Jackson Counties voted to secede, whereas a few representatives from proslavery areas like Berkeley, Jefferson, Hampshire, and Kanawha Counties voted no. When those who opposed secession returned home, to counties like Preston or Harrison or Marion or Ohio, they encountered pro-Union sentiments and large public gatherings.

At Clarksburg on April 22, John Carlile of Harrison County called for a Unionist convention to gather in Wheeling on May 13. This was the First Wheeling Convention: for three days, 425 delegates from 25 counties considered what kinds of actions to take against the growing secessionist sentiment in the eastern environs of the Old Dominion.

The largest delegations hailed from Wood and Marshall Counties (70 and 69 respectively), and the four Panhandle counties sent 155 men to Wheeling (37% of the total). The southern and southeastern parts of present-day West Virginia had no representation. Historians agree that the First Wheeling Convention "cannot be regarded as fully representative" of a state which in 1861 consisted of 150 counties and a future state which contained 50 counties upon its entrance into the federal union.

On May 14, Delegate Carlile, considered more radical than most of his colleagues, addressed the Secession Ordinance. "Let us repudiate these monstrous usurpations; let us show our loyalty to Virginia and the Union; and let us maintain ourselves in the Union at every hazard." His solution: creation of New Virginia. Other delegates, notably J.J. Jackson of Wood County, Waitman Willey of Monongalia, and Francis H. Pierpont of Marion, advised against any "premature" and "unwise" action until Virginian voters made their collective decision at the May 23 election. The convention postponed action on Carlile's motion but established a committee to draft an anti-secessionist response and to urge voters to cast ballots against secession on May 23.

With "three hearty cheers for the Union" the Convention adjourned, sine die, but in a "perfect blaze of enthusiasm." Those cheers soon turned to sighs: voters in northwestern counties heeded the pleas expressed in "To the People of North-Western Virginia," but the total vote, at least according to Richmond officials, was 125,950 to 20,373 in favor of Virginia's secession. Westerners cried foul: returns from 37 counties in the west were never included the final tally!

The *Wellsburg Herald* detailed the vote and showed the gulf which separated the Panhandle counties from the Tidewater:

COUNTY	FOR SECESSION	AGAINST SECESSION
Hancock	23	658
Brooke	109	721
Ohio	159	3156
Marshall	142	1993

First Convention members pledged to return to Wheeling if state voters approved the Secession Ordinance, and the Second Wheeling Convention convened on June 11. Like its predecessor, the Second Convention was unrepresentative of the proposed new state's counties: only 30 counties sent delegates, a figure that represented only one-fifth of the state.

Washington Hall, at the Corner of Market and Monroe (now 12th) Streets, held the first session, where Arthur I. Boreman of Wood County accepted the presidency of the convention with these words: "In this convention we have no ordinary political gathering. We have no ordinary task before us. We come here to carry out and execute, and it may be, to institute a government for ourselves.

We are determined to live under a State Government in the United States of America and under the Constitution ... [and] we have the stout hearts and the men who are determined in this purpose."

Two days later, on June 13, the Convention moved to the third floor courtroom of the Custom House, where John Carlile presented "A Declaration of the People of Virginia." This document called for "the reorganization of the government of the Commonwealth" and labeled "all acts ... tending to separate this Commonwealth from the United States, or to levy and carry on war against them ... without authority and void; and the offices ... vacated."

A day later, Carlile moved "an Ordinance for the Reorganization of State Government." To be sure, this action was a retreat from Carlile's proposal to create New Virginia, made during the First Convention, but its intent was to achieve the same end: a new state. Moreover, this action was necessary to comply with Article IV, Section 3 of the United States Constitution: "no new state shall be formed or erected within the jurisdiction of any other state ... without the consent of the legislatures concerned as well as of the Congress."

Most Virginians in 1861 did not want a new state to be carved from the Old Dominion, but the Second Convention's members did not represent their views. Rather, they advanced their own agenda, because they believed that separation was inevitable. The *Daily Intelligencer* supported these actions. "No man who recognizes the supremacy of the federal Constitution can question the political or moral right of the convention ... [to] establish a new state government."

But thousands of western Virginians did question the "right" of the Second Convention: they joined the Confederate armies; they refused to send delegations to Wheeling; and they would later refuse to vote for ratification of the ordinance to reorganize Virginia and then to create a new state. Those who failed to oppose the doings at the Second Convention were dealt a fait accompli. The *North West Commercial Advertiser* said it best: "Western Virginia, with its progressive and tolerant ideas, is henceforth to be the state!

Again, without any voter participation, the Second Convention installed state officers: Francis H. Pierpont, Governor; Daniel Polsley, Lt. Governor; and James Wheat, Attorney General. Governor Pierpont acknowledged the extraordinary nature of reorganization. "We are," he averred, "but recurring to the great fundamental principle of our fathers that to the loyal people of a state belong the law-making power of the State."

During July, the Assembly of Reorganized Virginia convened, and its first important action was to select new senators: Carlile and Willey were sent to Washington and were seated, but only after some debate and modest opposition. Secondly, the Assembly considered the question of creating a new state, and after some discussion in which members could not agree to the status of slavery in any future state, the matter was referred back to the Convention.

The Adjourned Session of the Second Wheeling Convention began the dismemberment of the Old Dominion. On August 20, delegates voted 48 to 27 to create a new state; the bill carried the title "An Ordinance to Provide for the Formation of a New State out of a Portion of the Territory of this State." This new state, if approved by voters in a referendum on October 24, would be called Kanawha.

Voters at that election agreed to the new state and elected delegates to the First Constitution Convention; its first meeting took place in the Wheeling Custom House on November 26. As with the First and Second Wheeling Conventions, selection of delegates was again problematic: several counties had no representatives; eight counties sent men whose elections were the result of military interference or work of the Methodist Episcopal Church; and in the case of Pocahontas County, the delegate was selected by "refugees" in Upshur County. Moreover, the number of voters who participated in that fateful October election was pitifully small: only 19,189 citizens cast ballots. Yet, the total population of those counties exceeded 376,000.

Constitutional Convention attendees first decided to change the state's name. Because the state contained a county and a river both named Kanawha, other names were proposed: Allegheny, Western Virginia, Augusta, and West Virginia. The latter garnered 30 votes; the total for the four other choices was only 14. Surprisingly, Northern Panhandle members were not strong in support of a new name: three from Ohio County voted for Kanawha; the Hancock County man voted for Allegheny; but the delegates from Brooke and Marshall voted for West Virginia.

In deciding the proper borders of their new state, delegates made sure that all of the counties over which passed the B&O Railroad were included.

Much debate centered on the issue of slavery. Surprisingly, many of these new West Virginians wanted to retain the "peculiar institution," but abolitionists among them, notably Gordon Battelle of Ohio County, pushed for gradual emancipation. In the end, the constitution contained no provision for abolition, allowing slavery to continue with this caveat: "No slave shall be brought, or free person of color be permitted into this state for permanent residence."

The constitution was passed with no dissenting votes cast, and the ratification was set for April 3, 1862. Like previous votes, this one too was overwhelmingly in support of a new constitution: 18,862 to 514 to ratify, and like previous election days, votes were not cast "in whole counties in the central, southern, and eastern parts of the proposed state." Nevertheless, the Reorganized Assembly met in May to continue its work for the citizens: on May 13, the Assembly approved the creation of the new state. Governor Pierpont chastised those who questioned or opposed the Assembly's direction as not understanding "the history, geography and social relation of our State." He continued, "If we could only get rid of the vast herd of the leaders of the State and get their lands into the hands of honest, working men, I predict for the State a prosperity unexampled in its history."

Senator Waitman Willey introduced the statehood-enabling act in the United States Senate on May 29, and debate continued into the summer. The question of slavery divided the Senate, but Willey's Amendment, which called for gradual emancipation, allowed the bill to be brought to the floor. The Senate passed the bill by a margin of 23 to 17, but eight Senators did not vote, meaning, of course, that a minority of the Senate approved the admission of West Virginia. One of those 17 no votes came from Senator John Carlile, the man who called for a "New Virginia" at the First Wheeling Convention in May 1861. He was the leader the *Intelligencer* once considered the best choice to fashion a new state out of the Old Dominion. Why he reneged is still a mystery to most historians, but the day was saved by Senator Willey, whom the *Intelligencer* opposed for election to the United States Senate, editorializing that he was "not, never was, nor never will be a leader," because "he [had] not the back bone for times like these."

Willey's Republican colleagues supported the work of the Wheeling Conventions reluctantly. Thaddeus Stevens of Pennsylvania stated, "I will not stultify myself by supposing that we have any warrant in the Constitution for this processing ... [for we admit] under an absolute power which the laws of war give us." James G. Blaine of Maine, a graduate of Washington & Jefferson College only 30 miles east of Wheeling and a future Republican Presidential standard bearer (1884), laid it on the line: "essentially the government of West Virginia was giving permission to the formation of a new state of West Virginia."

The House of Representatives delayed their vote until December, when on the 10th, after two days of spirited debate, the measure was approved by a vote of 96 to 55.

When the bill reached the White House, President Lincoln sought guidance from his cabinet. Attorney General Edward W. Bates proved the most ardent opponent. Formerly he described the actions of the Reorganized Government to dismember Virginia as "an original independent act of Revolution," and he called the enabling act for West Virginia "by its own intrinsic demerits, highly inexpedient [and] unconstitutional."

Lincoln ignored his Attorney General's advice and signed the bill on December 31, 1862, calling it "an expedient act." He added, "it is our secession ... secession in favor of the Constitution." Lincoln's signature was not the final chapter of this statehood saga. Admission would come only if West Virginians ratified a constitution that included the Willey Amendment.

The Constitution Convention met in a recalled session on February 12, 1863, and Senator Willey was there to defend his amendment and discuss the impact of Freedmen on a postwar economy of the state and the matter of compensation for slave owners. On February 17, the delegates accepted the Willey Amendment by unanimous vote, and, on the next day, without dissent, approved the amended constitution. Voters had their say on March 26, approving the changes by a margin of 27,749 to 572, despite Senator Carlile's continued efforts to defeat it. Certified election results allowed President Lincoln to issue the proclamation that admitted West Virginia as the nation's 35th state on June 20, 1863.

Detractors continued to express opposition. The Boston Commonwealth called the entire statehood proceedings bogus, and the New Jersey Legislature passed a resolution voicing its opposition to West Virginia's admission.

The Wheeling Conventions created a new state, one that could have only come to life in time of war. Lincoln admitted as much when he wrote that admission of West Virginia is not "a precedent for times of peace." During his Inaugural Address, Governor Arthur I. Boreman reaffirmed this belief, describing the new state as "the child of rebellion."

If there had not been a Civil War, there never would have been a West Virginia; if the Wheeling Conventions had been delayed, even by a few months, there would be no West Virginia; and if

128

all the counties currently in the Mountain State had had a voice in the proceedings and ratifications, there would not be a West Virginia. Finally, in this writer's opinion, if those conventions had met somewhere else, there would be no West Virginia. Wheeling is rightly called the birthplace of West Virginia, and considering this history of its creation, it should surprise no one that West Virginians call their state "Wild and Wonderful."

Often called the "Father of West Virginia," Francis H. Pierpont served as the Governor of the Restored State of Virginia from 1861 to 1863. Following West Virginia's official statehood, Arthur I. Boreman was elected Governor, and Pierpont established the government of the "restored" Virginia in Alexandria until the end of the war. In his later retirement, he helped create the West Virginia Historical Society. *(The History and Government of West Virginia by Richard Ellsworth Fast, 1901)*

July 1863

By Seán P. Duffy

July 1863 was an eventful month. The Battle of Gettysburg, the watershed engagement of the Civil War, spanned the first three days. Robert E. Lee withdrew in defeat from Pennsylvania just as, 1000 miles to the southwest in Mississippi, Confederate forces were dealt a second mortal blow as Grant accepted Pemberton's surrender at Vicksburg. Meanwhile, a New York City mob composed primarily of Irish immigrants enraged about the unfairness of the draft laws, rioted, violently attacking any African Americans in their path. Just days later, the 54th Massachusetts, an African American regiment, lost one third of their number in a courageous frontal assault on Fort Wagner in Charleston, South Carolina.

Throughout the month, Confederate cavalry under the command of John Hunt Morgan created quite a stir in the western border-states with a desperate raid (essentially a horse-thieving bender) covering 1000 miles from Tennessee, through Kentucky, Indiana, and Ohio.

By July 6, the *Daily Intelligencer*'s headlines were celebratory. "Glorious News. Defeat of Lee...Backbone of the Rebellion Broken at Last." Two days later, Wheeling learned of a second long-awaited victory. "Vicksburg has surrendered...Never were more glorious tidings borne over the wires...Truly last Saturday was a 4th of July second only to that of 1776."

The *Wheeling Register* went to press for the first time on July 10 as a new West Virginia flag flew over Linsly Institute, the temporary state capitol. An African American refugee from the New York riots named Solomons appeared in Wheeling with his girlfriend, whose head was wrapped to cover "a wound received by a flying missile." They had stopped on their way to a new life in Ohio.

While the people of Wheeling saw the mixed bag of distant events like Gettysburg, Vicksburg, and the New York riots through the confusing prism of newspaper reports, the Morgan raiders rode terrifyingly close to home. Despite this proximity, however, the story remained frustratingly (and somewhat comically) out of focus.

Perhaps to provide focus amid the chaos of war, riots, and raids, local pundits daily warned about an insidious, mustachio-twirling villain called "Copperheadism." Nationally, the term applied mostly to northern "Peace Democrats" (followers of Clement Vallandigham), but locally, the title was applied to just about anyone who expressed even the slightest doubt about the war. Copperheadism was soon equated with treason and used to explain bad news, from the New York riots (a copperhead plot to create a diversion for the rebels) to the Morgan Raids (abetted by Ohio copperheads).

Copperheads or "butternuts" lurked around every corner in the Ohio Valley. A trio of Wetzel county horse thieves confined in Wheeling's military prison, the Athenaeum, were said to have eyes "as green as grass...[probably] caused by the venom which belongs to the more dangerous species of the Copperhead..." Though not all were green-eyed rebels, horse thieves were regularly dragged to the Athenaeum. In fact, copperhead-perpetrated-horse-thievery became so pervasive that Senator Hawkins inquired about the expediency of making horse theft punishable by death.

But no horse thief dominated the local headlines in July 1863 quite like John Hunt Morgan. On July 20, Governor Boreman received a dispatch claiming that Morgan was trying to cross the Ohio River near Parkersburg. So began a head-spinning series of reports about the mercurial Morgan's mysterious whereabouts. "Ubiquitous John," was seemingly crossing into West Virginia simultaneously from almost every town on the Ohio River from Steubenville to Marietta.

Morgan hysteria gripped Wheeling. "Be Ready for Morgan," the *Intelligencer* admonished. "Every man who can shoot should have a gun [and] be ready at the ringing of the bells to rally at the Court House...Fellow Citizens...keep your powder dry." Two pieces of artillery and two companies of militia from Carlin's Wheeling Battery were promptly "planted in a position for service" on Wheeling Island. Even the *Intelligencer*'s staff stood ready.

"We are all able-bodied men at Quincy and Main and...we all hold ourselves ready to drop our pens...and shoulder our muskets."

On July 25 Morgan was reported to be in the nearby Ohio towns of St. Clairsville, then Moorefield, Senecaville, and Cadiz. Yet another witness was certain he had already crossed the river. So the bells were rung and the militia assembled at the Court House. Even Wheeling's older men were armed, including clergy like Rev. J.T. McLure and Rev. Mr. Barnes.

Perhaps the most over-the-top example, the so-called "Gunboat Expedition" left dock on July 25. "The [steamboat] *Wm. H. Harrison* under the command of Col. Darr and Capt. Moore left the wharf [with] two pieces of cannon and a couple hundred militia, including the members of the legislature [and the aforementioned clergymen], all well-armed." They steamed to intercept Morgan at the mouth of Short Creek, then above Steubenville. Alas, Morgan remained elusive.

The corporeal Morgan and his raiders were finally, actually defeated at Salineville, Ohio on July 26. Yet, even as shackles were being applied to the "Thunderbolt of the Confederacy," another dispatch was received claiming that Morgan was in Harrisville, Ohio and making his way to Wheeling.

Finally convinced that the danger had passed, the Wheeling militia marched to the Island where they discharged their weapons into the river, a "necessary precaution against accidents." Unfortunately, "many of the men held their muskets too high and...a great many bullets entered the houses in Bridgeport and Kirkwood, creating great alarm among the people."

For newspapermen, Morgan's Raid was just another symptom of pandemic Copperheadism. "If citizens want Morgan raids stopped they must not have sympathy with Morgan's cause," they wrote. "We will have raids...just as long as rebels of the south, encouraged by copperheads of the north, shall entertain hopes of...demoralization in the loyal states."

At the end of July, John Morgan arrived by train in Columbus, where he was to be imprisoned. As he stepped onto the platform, the crowd greeted him with a chant of "Horse Thief!" The chant grew louder as more people recognized him. "It is said," the newspapers reported, "that John Morgan actually shed tears."

A raid led by Confederate General John Hunt Morgan covered a region that extended from Tennessee to Ohio - the farthest north any uniformed Confederate troops penetrated during the war. Before he was captured, there were fears that he was headed for Wheeling. *(Library of Congress)*

August 2013
By Jon-Erik Gilot

By August 1, 1863, it seemed as though Wheeling residents could at long last breathe a sigh of relief. July had been taxing on the nerves – battles, raids, and riots dominated the headlines for much of the month. Wheeling soldiers had figured prominently throughout the Gettysburg campaign, and a number of African Americans recruited just across the river in Belmont and Jefferson counties had participated in the devastating assault on Fort Wagner. Ethnic tensions in New York City had boiled over into a deadly riot, and John Hunt Morgan's Confederate cavalry had come dangerously close to Wheeling before finally being captured in late July. Surely August would offer a reprieve.

Militarily speaking, August was a quiet month compared to what July had offered and what September was bound to bring. The Army of the Potomac and Army of Northern Virginia would jockey for position along the Rapidan and Rappahannock rivers. Federal forces around Charleston, South Carolina, initiated a prolonged bombardment of Confederate fortifications ringing Charleston Harbor, including the famed Fort Sumter. On August 21, Confederate partisan William Clarke Quantrill and his guerilla band sacked Lawrence, Kansas, killing more than 180 civilian men and boys and burning much of the town. Three years earlier Quantrill perpetrated what was perhaps the first of his many murders when he shot Chalkley Lipsey, who had been born near Wheeling in 1838.

More than military events, news of the unrelenting heat dominated the headlines in August of 1863. Thermometers stood near 100° in the shade through most of the month as swarms of flies tormented civilians and animals alike. On August 29th the *Intelligencer* reported large dust clouds blowing through the city as well as a noticeable green hue to the river. The warm days paired with little rain had caused the Ohio River to drop down to nearly just 20 inches, effectively shutting down river commerce. Hot days were exacerbated by a depleting supply of ice within the city. It was noted that since April more than 15 tons of ice had "disappeared" before being used.

The provost guard conducted a brisk business during the month of August. The government was offering $10 for each deserter arrested, and subsequently the Athenaeum was quickly filled with horse thieves and those soldiers who had absented themselves from their command. On August 22, the *Intelligencer* reported a gang of six Knights of the Golden Circle from Marshall County as having been arrested and confined in the Athenaeum. The Knights of the Golden Circle (KGC) was a secret society associated with Copperhead and pro-Confederate movements in northern states. One *Intelligencer* writer bemoaned the fact that no less than twenty requests had been received from ladies wishing to visit some of Morgan's raiders jailed in the Athenaeum, while no requests were received to visit the Union soldiers jailed there.

Two cases from the Athenaeum merited particular attention during the month. On August 2, it was reported that John Houston, a native of Washington County, Pennsylvania, and deserter from the Ringgold Cavalry, had apparently been attempting an escape when he was shot by Samuel Coats, a guard at the jail. The motive for the shooting was immediately called into question and, while the case was investigated, Coats was himself jailed at the Athenaeum, where he would remain until April of 1864. Houston was buried in the city cemetery.

In mid-August another Federal deserter, G.W. Thompson, was captured in Bridgeport and jailed in the Athenaeum. Thompson was apparently a notorious character, having previously escaped captors numerous times, even going so far as to jump out of a moving train. Later in the month Thompson would send a letter to the *Intelligencer* wherein he refuted some of the information published about him, complaining that he had been "sacrificed on the altar of newspaperdom." While he admitted to jumping out of the train, Thompson stated the train had been stationary, not moving.

We can't be sure, but perhaps the month of August gave Wheeling residents some hope. Abraham Lincoln had declared

August 6 a national day of Thanksgiving following the Federal victories of July, allowing for some hope that the Union might yet prevail. In mid-August the B&O railroad reopened a direct route from Baltimore to Wheeling, reinvigorating farmers and merchants who relied on the railroad for business and trade. During August the citizens of Wheeling held a festival in honor of Carlin's Battery, which raised enough money to purchase new instruments for the battery band. Those members of the battery who had been captured at the battle of Winchester were scheduled to be exchanged in late August, giving mothers hope that their sons might yet return home.

Unfortunately, any hope aroused in August would be dashed in September, which would bring more reverses for the Union and one of the costliest battles of the war.

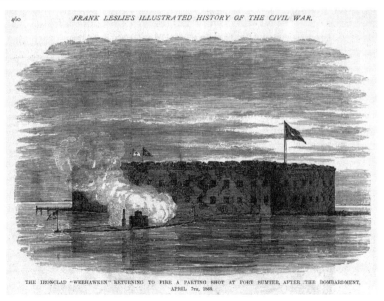

FRANK LESLIE'S ILLUSTRATED HISTORY OF THE CIVIL WAR.

THE IRONCLAD "WEEHAWKEN" RETURNING TO FIRE A PARTING SHOT AT FORT SUMTER, AFTER THE BOMBARDMENT, APRIL 7TH, 1863.

Constructed in 1829 as a coastal garrison, Ft. Sumter is most well known as having been the site of the first shots fired the Civil War on April 12, 1861. Following that attack, Confederate forces occupied the fort for nearly four years, despite Union efforts to recapture it. This image is from an unsuccessful, seven-day Union bombardment in 1863. (*Frank Leslie's Illustrated History of the Civil War*)

September 1863

By Joseph Laker

September 1863 began with Union advances against the Confederacy on many different fronts. The naval blockade of Confederate ports tightened, and Mobile, Alabama, and Fort Smith, Arkansas, were taken. While Union forces skirmished often but with little success against Lee's army in northern Virginia, Union armies advanced into eastern Tennessee with Gen. Ambrose Burnside occupying Knoxville and Gen. William Rosecrans seizing Chattanooga, then moving into Georgia. All went well until the Battle of Chickamauga on September 19-21, when Gen. Braxton Braggs' Confederates defeated Rosecrans forces. The Confederates laid siege to both Union armies, and for a time it appeared both might be lost. Placed in charge of all operations in the West, Ulysses Grant reinforced the Union army in Chattanooga with 15,000 soldiers from the northeast, most of whom traveled through Benwood and Wheeling by rail. Reinforced, the Union armies broke the sieges by the end of the year.

Along West Virginia's eastern border a series of hard fought campaigns took place between August and December. General William Averill began a Union raid into Confederate territory that resulted in the battle of Rocky Gap on August 26 and 27. Averill had been ordered to seize the law library in Lewisburg for use by the West Virginia legislature in Wheeling. He failed to achieve his main objective and had to retreat due to an insufficient number of men and ammunition. The Union lost 27 killed, 125 wounded, and 67 missing; Confederates suffered 20 dead, 129 wounded and 18 missing. Wheeling men were among those killed and wounded. A detailed account of the campaign, written by the chaplain of the 3rd West Virginia Mounted Infantry, appeared in the *Daily Intelligencer* on September 10th, a week before Averill sent in his own battle report. The chaplain was highly critical of the Union commanders for many reasons, but especially for beginning the campaign without adequate ammunition, horseshoes, and nails and launching attacks on the morning of August 27th, before retreating.

The chaplain was placed under arrest by General Averill, after his account appeared.

Union woes continued. Early in the morning of September 12th, Confederates under John Hanse McNeill overran five companies of Union troops at Moorefield resulting in the death, wounding, or capture of almost 230 men. Again, Wheeling men were among those lost.

While Wheeling remained relatively untouched by wartime violence there were lots of riots, beatings, robberies, and murders in nearby areas carried out by bushwackers (rebel guerrillas) and undisciplined Union soldiers. At the end of September a civilian, James Frazier, got into a quarrel with a soldier in the Cambridge, Ohio, train station. Frazier fled to his brother Tom's store with 30 soldiers in pursuit. There, the argument resumed and led to the wounding of two soldiers. The Frazier brothers fled to a house a half mile away, but the soldiers followed and killed Tom; James escaped.

Late on the evening of September 21, thirty rebels arrived at the home of the Glaze family in Roane county looking for Union soldiers home on leave and murdered four men they found in an out building, but several escaped to raise the alarm. The next day Union troops caught up with some of the band and killed two of them. The article in the *Daily Intelligencer* ended with the observation "It is thought there can be no peace in Roane county until one or other of the parties is extinguished. They cannot live together."

At the end of September the *Daily Intelligencer* discussed the arrest of two men who had left Union held parts of Virginia at the beginning of the war and returned home in the summer of 1863. The article ended with the comment, "the country is full of this class of persons, who are spies, and we advise the people to hunt them up and shoot them as they would panthers."

Crime and violence in Wheeling weren't only committed by soldiers passing through. Two West Virginia legislators were victims of burglary at their respective hotels, a drowned male infant was pulled from the river by a big dog, and a week later a local man found a two-week old female infant who had been abandoned on top of a coal shed. The well-dressed female infant had an extra set of clothes laid beside her. The baby survived. The newspapers mentioned other murders, shoplifting, etc. Mischievous young boys were accused of putting firecrackers on a drunk man and tying a hot coffee pot to the tail of a dog.

Both houses of the West Virginia legislature met in Wheeling during the month of September and debated and passed legislation including setting up a system to regulate physicians through licensure, a confiscation law permitting the government to seize the property of West Virginians convicted of aiding the rebellion, financing road construction, and restructuring electoral districts. Both Unionists, associated with the Republican Party, and Peace Democrats carried out political rallies.

August and September in 1863 saw little rainfall. The river level stayed consistently below two feet in the main channel, and river traffic was possible only for the smallest of steamboats. However, the Baltimore and Ohio railroad reopened to full operations after having been partially shut down by Confederate raids. Wheeling remained prosperous, and with the West Virginia legislatures meeting daily, there was much activity in town. Entertainment was provided by the Sanford Minstrels, who played to packed houses at Washington Hall from September 7th through the 12th. The troupe offered comic skits, music, and several burlesque plays, including an Ethiopian Opera. A week after the minstrels left for Pittsburgh, Professor Anderson and his wife Marian arrived for a week's stint at Washington Hall. The Andersons gave lectures and conducted experiments to entertain their audiences. He was a magician and an escape artist. One stunt had him bound hand and foot by members of the audience, briefly covered by a cloak, and when the cloak was taken off he was free, but the knots were still tied.

Troops from the surrounding region mustered in Wheeling and then were sent to strategic locations either by rail or boat. This image shows soldiers ready to board steamboats in Benwood. *(Frank Leslie's Illustrated History of the Civil War)*

October 1863
By Jeanne Finstein

Upcoming Congressional elections were in the Wheeling news during the early days of October 1863 as the war continued on both the eastern and western fronts. Although Wheeling's Chester D. Hubbard was seen as being "instrumental in convincing Lincoln of the necessity of signing the statehood bill," Parkersburg's Jacob B. Blair received the first district nomination instead. Daniel Frost also agreed to run for Congress, from the third district. Frost was born in St. Clairsville and had served as editor of the Union-leaning *Virginia Chronicle* in Ravenswood, until Confederates burned his paper. He was elected Speaker of the House in the Restored Government of Virginia and then enlisted in the 11th West Virginia Infantry, serving with distinction. The *Intelligencer* described his opponent, K. V. Whaley, as "loyal, after a fashion" but "absolutely no account at all." Despite this and other criticism of Whaley, he defeated Frost. Unfortunately, Frost was never able to reach his potential in politics; he was killed in action at the Battle of Snicker's Ferry in July 1864.

Newspaper notice was given on October 1 alerting relatives that Jacob Hornbrook would be returning to Wheeling the next day with local soldiers' pay. Nicknamed the "soldier's friend," Hornbrook had distinguished himself in business and as a delegate to the First Wheeling Convention, urging statehood. Although considered too old to serve in the military, he took it upon himself to travel the countryside to where Wheeling soldiers were stationed, often accompanied by his daughter India (daughter-in-law of General Benjamin Franklin Kelley), to bring home the soldiers' pay, ensuring that their dependents were taken care of in their absence. On this particular trip, the amount he brought back from the 1st, 14th, and 15th regiments was reported to have been between $25,000 and $30,000 (the equivalent of about $450,000 to $550,000 today).

The first term of the Ohio County Circuit Court in the new state of West Virginia was held early in October and included the trial of James Collins, accused of the murder of John W. Lewis. Reports of the trial testimony were apparently of great interest, given the amount of newspaper coverage. A scathing editorial followed the jury's finding of justifiable homicide. Lesser altercations also made the news, including one case in which a fight erupted when one man called the other a "son of a female dog" and was insulted in return by being called a Confederate.

A daily summary of war news was typically printed on page 3 of the paper, and a list of names of local casualties periodically appeared. A huge crowd attended an address given in Wheeling by General Franz Sigel on October 14, and Union rallies and processions were held frequently. Also in mid month was an announcement that there were to be no through trains to Baltimore due to an "apprehended danger of a raid beyond Cumberland." Meanwhile, the West Virginia legislature appropriated $2000 to pay the expenses of bringing wounded and sick soldiers home from distant hospitals or battlefields and returning the remains of the fallen when friends and family could not afford the expense of transportation.

The role of slaves freed by President Abraham Lincoln was still uncertain, even though nearly a year had passed since the Emancipation Proclamation. One outlandish rumor was that Lincoln would "enforce amalgamation by conscripting a large number of young white ladies who would be compelled to accept husbands from the black brigade." The same *Intelligencer* issue included statements by a Louisiana legislator that "the slaves of the South [are] more intelligent and capable of sustaining a representative government than the peasantry in many states of Europe" and that there was "hardly a plantation on the Mississippi which did not have upon it some slave who knew more about its management than his master."

A week later, a reprint of an article from the southern-leaning *Richmond Enquirer* expressed dismay that [former] slave owners were averse "to hire their negroes in the Confederate army. The prejudice is certainly an ignorant and mean one. As the war was originated and is carried out in part for the defense of the slaveholder and his property, rights, and the perpetuation of the institution, it is reasonable to suppose that he ought to be the first and foremost in aiding the triumph and success of our arms. Good wages are offered, and proper care and attention will be given every negro hired to the army, and the slaveholder ought to remember that for every negro he thus furnishes, he puts a soldier in the ranks."

Advertisements, often found on the front page of the paper, reflect the general war environment. For example, D. Nicoll & Bro, 109 Main Street, advertised the receipt of 100 dozen Union flags, and patent medicines focused on the needs of soldiers. Ads for Hoofland's German Bitters (75-cents per bottle, with "no alcohol or bad whisky") told those who had friends in the army that the product would "cure nine tenths of the diseases induced by exposure and privations incident to camp life." Another option, the "Never Known to Fail, Soldier's Friend, Dixon's Blackberry Carminative" claimed to be the "sovereign remedy for dysentery, diarrhea, flux, cholera morbus, and summer complaint." On a more ominous note, the Geo. R. Taylor store announced the receipt of a new shipment of "mourning goods."

Women's fashion news appeared frequently in the newspaper. The season's bonnets were to have more shallow sides and drooping fronts than those in the prior season. Light and gauzy fabrics for dresses were being replaced with "heavy merinos and dark silk" for fall. And although the belt waist was still in fashion, a more pointed waist could be seen "on the promenade." Skirts retained "full flowing amplitude of width" and were often trimmed with broad bands of velvet placed horizontally, vertically, or diagonally. A later report praised the latest Paris fashions that shortened skirts to a point that they no longer featured the "filthy and extravagant" lengths that swept the streets and brought dust into houses...This change in fashion is one of the most sensible we have yet had occasion to record."

Daniel Frost was editor of the Union-leaning Ravenswood *Virginia Chronicle* before the Civil War. He became the Speaker of the House for the Restored Government of Virginia but then volunteered for military service and was commissioned as lieutenant colonel. His two younger brothers fought for the Confederacy. Frost was mortally wounded in the Battle of Snicker's Ferry. He was buried in Mt. Wood Cemetery. *(Photo by Jeanne Finstein)*

November 1863
By Joseph Laker

November 1863 was a time of much and varied military activity throughout the nation. Although intense fighting took place in northern Virginia, no breakthrough was made. The northern navy reduced Fort Sumter in Charleston, South Carolina's harbor to rubble with bombardments that had lasted more than 130 days, but still could not seize the fort. However, Gen. Ulysses Grant's victory at Chattanooga opened Georgia to invasion by Northerners and Gen. William Averill's victory over the Confederates at Droop Mountain ended any significant threat to West Virginia. Canadians suppressed a plot by Confederates to launch an attack on Johnson Island in Ohio where the Union held 3,000 rebels.

The most important national political event during the month was the dedication of Gettysburg cemetery on November 19th. With 19 states contributing money, Pennsylvania's Governor Andrew G. Curtin purchased the 17-acre site. The day was sunny, but there was a cold biting wind. Following the parade from town, the Chaplain of the House of Representatives offered a long prayer, the Marine band played a tune called "Old Hundredth," and then the featured speaker, Edward Everett, gave a two hour and five minute speech. Following another song, the President was introduced and gave his now famous Gettysburg Address. It took just five minutes, and Lincoln had finished and resumed his seat before the photographer had a chance to snap his picture at the rostrum. National reactions to the President's remarks were mixed. Few saw it as a masterpiece, but Everett told Lincoln at the time that it was perfect.

The governor of each state in the Union had been invited to the ceremony. The West Virginia delegation left Wheeling on the B & O on November 17th and was made up of Governor Arthur Boreman, two generals, three politicians, and Archibald Campbell of the *Daily Intelligencer*. After spending the night in Harrisburg, the party took a train for Gettysburg, but the trip, expected to last three hours, took nine, and the trip was largely done without light, heat, or food; there were, however, plenty of alcoholic spirits to drink. The trip home was uneventful.

In Wheeling the Senate and House of Delegates considered more than 75 pieces of legislation, which ranged from organizing local government, schools, and the judiciary to one prohibiting the manufacturing of alcoholic beverages. (It failed.) One bill called for giving the state greater authority to confiscate and then sell the property of all citizens who committed treason against the state. Even before the passage of this confiscation bill, the state had seized the property of some who had joined the rebellion and the *Daily Intelligencer* ran advertisements for the sale of the property of eleven such individuals during November.

The *Daily Intelligencer* also kept the people of Wheeling informed about conditions in the Confederacy by printing information from intercepted rebel letters, interviews with rebel prisoners and northerners who had returned from the South, and reprints of articles from British, Northern, and Southern newspapers. During November it especially published articles from three Richmond papers: the *Enquirer*, *Examiner*, and *Whig*. The purposes of the articles were to buoy the supporters of the war effort as well as to provide information. Some of the problems Richmond papers covered were the decreasing value of Confederate currency, fears of slave revolts, the terrible treatment accorded Union men imprisoned in Richmond, food shortages, and rapidly climbing prices. On November 12, the *Daily Intelligencer* reported that in Richmond beans cost $18-20 a bushel, butter $3.50-4.00 a pound, corn meal $14.00-15.00 a bushel, and brandy $33.00-50.00 a gallon.

Paroled prisoners estimated that on average 43 prisoners a day died in Richmond prisons due to lack of adequate food, medicines, and clothing, and crowded living conditions. Wheeling citizens were urged to send aid boxes to Union prisoners in rebel hands via Adams Express. A list of the contents was to be included in the box, with copies sent separately to the recipient and to Brigadier General S. A. Marshall, who handled such aid transfers.

Wheeling remained prosperous, and the steamboat building industry was active, with boat prices and values rising rapidly. The *Tempest*, which sold for $3,500 in 1862, now brought $12,000 in Pittsburgh while a boat built for Captain Fowler, which had cost him $30,000, was sold for $42,000, still unfinished. The city purchased two new fire engines and incorporated a company to build a turnpike from Lydia Shepherd Cruger's home in Elm Grove to the Pennsylvania border by following Wheeling Creek. Not everyone in the city benefitted from the general prosperity, and particularly hard hit were families of soldiers. More than 120 families were found to be in dire need, and a citizens group was formed to raise $10,000 to provide them with assistance.

For those with money, entertainment available in Wheeling occurred at Washington Hall. For a week starting on Monday, November 2, people could pay 25 or 50 cents (regular or reserved seats) to see a panoramic painting "giving a complete history of the war from the bombardment of Fort Sumter to the capture of Vicksburg." The painting was accompanied by Rufus Somerby's patriotic lecture, while his wife sang songs appropriate to the different scenes. The event played to a packed house each evening. During the second half of the month two different troupes performed at Washington Hall. Hernandez Foster and his Star Troupe performed three plays: a drama, a farce, and a Negro Extravaganza called "Jumbo Jim." Then, the Zanfretta Family supplied music, dancing, acrobatics, contortionists, and high wire and trapeze acts.

Less pleasant entertainment was provided by the numerous drunk and disorderly persons who filled some city streets, counterfeiters and scam artists, robbers, and murderers. Even hogs were a problem, eating lots of grain standing in front of warehouses or on the wharf waiting for shipment. When one grain dealer shot and killed such a hog, he was fined $4.50 for discharging a weapon in the city and threatened with a lawsuit by the hog's owner.

Built in 1798, Monument Place was still occupied by the original owner, Lydia Boggs Shepherd Cruger, during the Civil War. She had been present at the second siege of Ft. Henry in 1782 and lived until 1867, age 101. During the war years, plans were made to improve the road between her house and the Pennsylvania line, most likely following the path of the National Road, which had reached Wheeling nearly 50 years before. *(Photo by Jeanne Finstein)*

December 1863
By Kate Quinn

As Wheeling area residents prepared to celebrate Christmas 1863, reports in the *Daily Intelligencer* reassured them that one threat that had existed for much of the Civil War – intervention on the side of the Confederacy by England and France – appeared to have ended. The *Intelligencer* stated, "We remain in peace and friendship with foreign powers. The efforts of disloyal citizens of the United States to involve us in foreign wars, to aid in inexcusable insurrection have been unavailing. Her Britannic Majesty's government, as was justly expected, have exercised their authority to prevent the departure of new hostile expeditions from British ports. The Emperor of France, as by a like proceeding, promptly indicated the neutrality which he proclaimed at the beginning of this contest."

Disputes between England and France notwithstanding, they at least did not interfere too much in our Civil War, except that England continued to allow the Confederacy to purchase ships that had been built there. The English also persisted in hampering the Union's blockade of shipping the vast amounts of cotton still produced in the South. They did at least sign a treaty for the suppression of the African slave trade on February 7, 1863, and ratified it in December. Perhaps Gov. Francis Pierpont's message to the Legislature in Alexandria was in point to remind them and the South that, "they have nothing to expect in the way of peace or prosperity until they get rid of the debris of slavery still left among them."

In that hope, a "Council of Thirty Three" (representing the 33 states still in the Union) was appointed by Congress to ascertain "what it was the Southern states actually wanted – free trade or slavery." An English statesman named Cobden commented, "The fact was it was the aristocracy of the South fighting against the democracy of the North."

Rebecca Harding Davis, Wheeling author of *Life in the Iron Mills*, published a short story called *Paul Blecker* in *Atlantic Monthly* in December 1863. This was the story of two sisters who strove to overcome life's hardships but in the end were dependent on the men they chose for satisfaction in life.

Robert Smalls, a 21-year-old enslaved wheelman, stole a Confederate ship (the *CSS Planter*), and taking the families of the other slaves of the ship aboard, sailed to Union ships blockading Charleston, South Carolina, where he not only turned over the ship but also the Confederate code book! He became a Northern hero and was influential in persuading President Lincoln to allow blacks to serve the Northern forces.

Since their three-year hitch was ending, soldiers were asked to re-enlist, and the draft was enacted. West Virginia Gov. Arthur I. Boreman placed an article on the front page of the *Daily Intelligencer* stating, "People of West Virginia, our armies are victorious on all points – a number of states and parts of states have been recovered from the dominion of the enemy and the rebellion is rapidly on the wane, yet a great work remains to be done. You have responded most nobly whenever called heretofore and I take great pride in saying that I have no fear of your failure on this occasion."

On a lighter note, life in Wheeling went on. The large number of pigs roaming the streets was called an "army of occupation" by a reporter. One pig entered a small home, found a bag of cornmeal under the bed, pulled it out to the street, and began to feast. A man passing by identified the meal as having been stolen from him the night before. The lady of the house confessed that her husband had stolen the grain out of need and then offered to pay the man for the meal. The report noted that the pig also belonged to the wronged gentleman and that the pig "had a nose for detective work."

The case of Thomas Higgs vs. John Goshorn over the sale of a young boy for $800 was noted by the newspaper as "probably the last negro sale case that will be heard in this city for several hundred years."

The *Daily Intelligencer* also described the city's store windows as showing dozens of toys, including one called a "dancing Johnny," a jointed figure of wood on strings. Also in vogue was a move called "the Grecian Wiggle." Ladies crossing gutters in hoop skirts were able, without touching their dresses, to "set the dress on a 45-degree angle on the right to the gutter and the Grecian part is to sling it 45 degrees to the left so as to escape the gutter. It is a beautiful movement uncommonly graceful, but it requires that a lady have no holes in her stockings."

Skating on Big Wheeling Creek was noted as a current recreational event. The reporter was astounded to see women partaking in the pastime but encouraged their efforts.

On the war front, 800 prisoners were exchanged at Fort Monroe, and Gen. William Averill's cavalry tore up the Tennessee and Virginia railroad line after fording freezing rivers and hauling artillery over mountains. They found Confederate stores of wheat, corn, oats, and flour, and then took 200 prisoners with a loss of only 60 men. Gen. William Rosecrans congratulated the West Virginia troops on this maneuver.

Harper's Weekly carried this poignant reminder, "Ought it not be a Merry Christmas? Even with all the sorrow that hangs over so many households; even while the war still rages; even while there are still serious questions yet to be settled – ought it not be, and is it not a Merry Xmas?" Since the streets of our city were littered with the remains of thousands of Jackson crackers (fireworks) the day after Christmas and reporters noted the teeming crowds of strolling citizens on the day, it seems that Wheeling did indeed have a Merry Christmas.

Rebecca Harding's family moved to Wheeling when she was a young girl. She lived in Centre Wheeling and wrote about the lives of marginalized people, such as blacks, women, Native Americans, immigrants, and the working class. Her most well known book was *Life in the Iron Mills*. She and her husband L. Clarke Davis were the parents of another successful author and journalist Richard Harding Davis. *(Ohio County Public Library Archives)*

January 1864
By Joseph Laker

January 1864 found most of the nation, including Wheeling, in the grip of a very cold and snowy winter. The Ohio River froze over bringing a halt to boat traffic for almost a month, and those who wanted to cross the river had to walk across the ice, a dangerous method of travel at both the start and end of the big freeze. While dozens of skirmishes occurred between the Union and Confederate armies, no significant battles took place during the month, and the severe cold hampered both sides.

Important national news centered around increased discussion in the North on how to treat the seceded states once Union forces achieved victory. In Arkansas citizens voted on a new pro-Union Constitution on January 19; three days later Isaac Murphy was chosen as provisional governor. In Union-controlled areas of Tennessee, people called for a constitutional convention and an end to slavery. Meanwhile, President Lincoln called for the continued payment of bounties to army volunteers, and in Congress the 13th amendment to the Constitution, which would end slavery, was proposed as a joint resolution.

In Wheeling the most important political issue of the month was the election of top city officials on January 25. The election was hotly contested between those who belonged to a conservative establishment, supported by the *Daily Register*, against a strongly pro-Unionists slate, supported by the *Daily Intelligencer*. Among the positions to be filled were mayor, city sergeant, treasurer, supervisor of water works, wharf master, and members of both houses of the City Council. In the 1860s Wheeling's city council was divided into two chambers, and important legislation had to pass both bodies to become law. The *Daily Intelligencer* exulted that the Unionist ticket was almost completely successful, yet complained that voters should be chastened that so many voted for the opposition and were ignorant or complicit with the disloyal. In January 1865 the election would swing the other way, and the Unionist candidates lost out. The *Daily Register* claimed that the

1864 election was flawed because some soldiers stationed at the Athenaeum, who were not citizens of Wheeling, were allowed to vote and that corruption marred the voting, especially in the fourth ward. The *Register* told the story of one young boy who had been sent by his grandfather to pick up a ballot that favored the establishment ticket and twice had his grandfather's ballot taken from him and replaced with a Unionist ballot. In each case supporters of the establishment slate intervened to make sure that the correct ballot was eventually cast.

A second election issue arose over who had the right to vote in the election. According to the city of Wheeling's regulations, all ballots had to be cast in person, so soldiers from Wheeling who could not be in the city for the election to personally cast their ballot were disenfranchised. But according to West Virginia's 1863 constitution, all cities and towns must permit citizens the opportunity to cast ballots in person or by mail. First, both chambers of the city council voted to follow the city's rules but then reversed that vote to follow the state constitution on January 23, only to change again the next day and require the voter to personally hand in his ballot. The *Daily Intelligencer* favored following the Constitution while the *Daily Register* vehemently supported the traditional procedure required by the city's rules.

On January 13 the Wheeling Board of Health issued its annual report on the causes of death during 1863. Of the 389 people who died, 208 were male, 176 were female, and for 5 the sex was not stated. More than 53% who died were five years of age or less. While 83 causes of death were listed, the most common were: inflammation of the lungs, cholera infantum, convulsions, softening of the brain, and diphtheria. Only three individuals were murdered. The report was less than clear on the cause of death of people like Casper Miller. The trial of Frederick Miller for the killing of Casper Miller (not related) concluded on January 8. Both men had worked at the Belmont Nail Works and on August 28, 2013 an argument had broken out when Frederick upset a wheelbarrow full of bricks that Casper was pushing. The men exchanged words and threw bricks at one another. Casper was struck in the forehead and died in September of swelling of the brain. The state put four witnesses on the stand, the defense eleven, most of whom were character witnesses. Joseph Vogler testified that he was at Casper's house the day he died and that Casper agreed to forgive Frederick and would shake his hand. Frederick came to Casper's home, but as Casper reached out his hand to Frederick he went into convulsions and passed away. After considering the case for 30 minutes the jury reached a verdict of not guilty.

There was considerable entertainment available to start the new year. A German concert and ball was held in Union Hall on New Years Eve. The Sanford troupe of comedians and musicians entertained at Washington Hall on January 1st and 2nd. Low-brow fare featuring the Townshead Exhibition at Washington Hall ran from January 6 through the 13th. For a cost of 15 cents one could see the 8-foot Arabian giant, the 400-pound Colossal Girl, a family of Albinos, a monster snake that was 20 feet long and 19 inches thick, and the Great Nondescript - yes, it is a mystery. High-brow fare followed on January 14th with a classical music concert featuring the famous Brignold and Gottshalk orchestra at Washington Hall. The Ramsey troupe performed on January 16 and 18 to cap the month's entertainment.

Both Wheeling newspapers gave extensive coverage of the escape of the Confederate raider John Hunt Morgan and a few of his fellow prisoners from Camp Chase in Columbus. The papers gave Morgan's own account of their tunneling out of the prison and escape to Dixie.

Located at the northeast corner of Market and Monroe Streets, now Market and 12th, Washington Hall was the site of the First Wheeling Convention, held May 13 - 15, 1861, and the beginning of the Second Wheeling Convention, which began on June 11. Due to space considerations, the delegates then moved to the courtroom of the Custom House to continue their deliberations. Washington Hall then returned to its previous use as a venue for performances and exhibitions. The building was erected in 1851 at a cost of $46,000 and opened in 1853. It was totally destroyed by fire in 1876. *(Ohio County Public Library Archives)*

February 1864
By Jon-Erik Gilot

The winter of 1864 had thus far proven to be a welcome respite from the many battles and hardships that would go down as the hallmark of 1863. Whereas February was typically a month of rest and recuperation for both armies, this month in 1864 saw a marked activity in military activity that helped to define not only the remainder of the year, but the war itself. February would see General William T. Sherman initiate what would become known as his "March Through Georgia." The march would actually begin in Mississippi, where Sherman captured Jackson and Meridian, and would take nearly a full year before Sherman emerged at Savannah, Georgia, on December 21, 1864.

On February 20, a small battle in Florida would have effects that would ripple back to the Ohio Valley. At Olustee, a Union force of 5,500 men (including many United States Colored Troops) lost roughly 35% of their number in fighting a similarly sized Confederate army. The 54th Massachusetts Infantry, recruited heavily in the Ohio Valley the previous year, figured prominently in the battle. While these local soldiers escaped from Olustee unscathed, that would not be the case later in the year at the battle of Honey Hill. On February 24 Congress voted to reinstate the rank of Lieutenant General, last held by George Washington. The rank would soon be conferred to Ulysses S. Grant, who had started the war as a simple recruiting officer. In the summer of 1864 Grant would initiate months of unrelenting bloodshed, adding exponentially to the war-weariness of the North while draining the manpower of the South.

On February 27 the first Union prisoners arrived at Camp Sumter, Georgia, later known as Andersonville. More than 45,000 Union prisoners, including many from Wheeling and the Ohio Valley, would pass through the gates of Andersonville during the next 15 months – nearly 13,000 of them remained at Andersonville, buried in the National Cemetery.

February was an eventful month in the city of Wheeling. Above average temperatures would fall drastically, not unlike the cold snaps recently experienced in our area. The *Intelligencer* bemoaned a scarcity of dwelling houses in the city. Rent prices had "gone up" with increased immigration to the city, not unlike the housing situation in Wheeling today.

February 1864 also saw the return of several of Wheeling's finest regiments – the 1st Cavalry, 1st Infantry, and 7th Infantry all reached the city after re-enlisting as veterans and earning a 30-day furlough. The regiments arrived with much pomp and circumstance – parades, bands, speeches and dinners. The celebrations were dimmed on February 20 when a local man was gravely injured by the premature explosion a cannon set to mark the arrival of the 1st West Virginia Infantry. Other regiments, including the 1st Light Artillery (Battery D) and the 15th Infantry, were in town on recruiting duty, trying hard to refill their ranks before the spring campaign.

Perhaps the greatest concern during the month of February was the government's latest call for troops. In October Lincoln had issued a call for 300,000 more men to serve in the Federal armies, and in February the call was revised to 500,000. Each county of each state was responsible for meeting a specific quota, based on the number of military-aged men living in the county who hadn't yet enlisted. If the quota numbers were not met with volunteers, a draft would be initiated. Ohio County's quota was 200 men.

Ohio County had already sent nearly 1,200 men to the war, while more than 3,000 men remained in the county who were eligible for a draft. For some reason these men weren't enlisting. Was it the fear of an agonizing death on a far away battlefield or hospital, far from loved ones and friends? This was not the case at all. To the dismay of Ohio County officials, these men were enlisting in droves, just not in the right county.

It came to the attention of the county officials that Brooke and Marshall Counties were offering bounties of up to $200 per enlistee on top of the government bounty. This bonus was drawing many Ohio County men outside county lines to enlist, thereby depopulating the number of men Ohio county could draw on to fill their quota with volunteer enlistments. The stigma of a "draft" in the capital county of the new state of West Virginia was becoming quite real. Something must be done.

A mass meeting was announced at the Ohio County courthouse for February 8, 1864. The patriotic meeting featured bands and many speeches by the mayor, the governor, and military officers, all calling on local men to answer their country's call and fill the quota. The county decided they would offer a $300 bounty to each enlistee, this on top of the $300 government bounty, and an additional $100 for veteran volunteers, bringing a total of up to $700 per enlistee.

By February 20 the 200-man quota for the county had been filled, mainly by residents of the border counties. Whereas Brooke and Marshall had been drawing on Ohio County recruits, Wheeling's new $300 bounty enticed men from the surrounding counties. Just as Wheeling had feared a draft for its county, Wellsburg and Moundsville now faced the same reality.

The money available to recruits in Wheeling in February of 1864 would be valued at over $10,000 in today's currency. That sum was more than what many Wheeling residents could earn in a year – and it was now available with the simple stroke of a pen. The money could do much to change the fortune of one's self or family. Unfortunately, many of those fortunes would change in a vastly different way in a hospital bed or on a battlefield far from Ohio County.

Several Wheeling soldiers had the misfortune of being sent to the horrific Andersonville Prison. Among them were several members of Carlin's Battery. Some died due to the harsh conditions; others survived the prison but died when the *Sultana* riverboat bringing them home exploded; and a few made it back to Wheeling. *(Library of Congress)*

March 1864

By John Bowman

On March 1, 1864 in the Eastern War Theater, Union General Hugh J. Kilpatrick and Colonel Ulric Dahlgren attempted an unsuccessful raid on the Confederate capital at Richmond. A few days earlier, General William Sherman in the Western Theater had concluded his successful raid on Meridian, Mississippi. Sherman's strategy was to speedily march an army through Confederate territory with impunity, feed it at the expense of its inhabitants, and do this with negligible losses to his army. This plan was the proving ground for Sherman's future "March to the Sea." A correspondent in Nashville reported, "Sherman found the country through which he passed abounds with all-life's necessaries for man and beast and he leaves the country perfectly impoverished wherever he has been." In contrast to this, much to Sherman's disgust, "A Confederate cavalry unit captured crewmembers from the Union tinclad *USS Rattler* attending church services at Rodney, Mississippi."

On March 8, the steamer *Anglo-Saxon*, with General Ulysses S. Grant aboard, docked at Wheeling, and he immediately boarded a train for Washington. Four days later, the *Daily Intelligencer* reported, "The President of the United States, this afternoon formally presented to Major General Grant his commission and superlative three-star rank of Lieutenant General and General-In-Chief of the Army of the United States." The President rose and addressed him thus, "General Grant, the nation's appreciation of what you have done, and its reliance on you for what needs to be done in the existing great struggle, are now presented with this commission."

On the same day, the *Intelligencer* reported, "The Provost Guard Quells the Disturbance. As has been the case almost every day for two weeks a big fight took place yesterday on Market Square [Market and 10th Streets] among some cavalry soldiers. A half a dozen fights appeared to be going on at the same time in different places, and several pistol shots were fired. The greatest alarm was created among the residents in the vicinity, and many people shut up their places of business. A half a dozen men were cut up, bruised, and bled profusely. A squad of the Provost Guard came up from the Athenaeum, the disorderly soldiers dispersed in various directions, and many concealed themselves, although several were arrested and committed to prison. One man who was recognized as a leading rioter, attempted to run away from the guard. He was several times halted while being pursued and would certainly have been killed but that the armed soldier nearest to him was fearful some innocent person on the sidewalk between himself and the fleeing man might be injured. The guard finally got a clear sight at the man and drew up his gun to shoot, but before doing so, the other halted and gave up. The proceedings were both disgraceful and alarming."

On March 13, the steamer *Anglo-Saxon* left Wheeling with General Grant aboard heading to Nashville. Grant had summoned General Sherman to meet him at Nashville on the 17th where they would discuss Sherman's plan of attack on General Joseph Johnston's Confederate Army, defensively dug in at Dalton, Georgia.

The *Intelligencer* quoted the War Department on March 16. "The President of the United States has made a call for two hundred-thousand men, in addition to the call of February 1st, 1864, for five hundred-thousand, subject to addition for deficiencies and deductions for excess on that quota. The quotas of the several counties of the First Congressional District will be as follows: Hancock 31, Wirt 92, Brooke 35, Ritchie 40, Ohio 205, Doddridge 41, Marshall 87, Harrison 137, Wetzel 46, Lewis 47, Tyler 43, Gilmer 8, Pleasants 36, Calhoun 15 and Wood 110, a total of 93l. No definite statement can be made until the returns of re-enlisted men are received." Signed James B. Fry, Provost Marshall General.

In Nashville on March 17, General Grant announced that General Sherman was to take command of the Military Division of Mississippi, embracing the Departments of the Ohio, Cumberland, Tennessee, and Arkansas and upon his, Grant's, returning to the

Eastern Theater, his Headquarters will be in the field with General George Meade's Army of the Potomac.

On March 18, Grant and Sherman boarded the *Anglo-Saxon* in Nashville and headed for Wheeling. During the voyage they discussed each of their subordinate generals' strengths and weaknesses and determined that if anything were to happen to either, Brigadier General James McPherson would be the likely one to succeed either. As to the furtherance of the war effort, Grant's broad strategy was, "Starting in May, he was to go for Lee and Sherman was to go for Johnston." Sherman left the boat at Cincinnati, boarded the steamer *Julia*, and headed back to Nashville. Grant continued on to Wheeling, quietly boarded the B&O, and arrived in Washington on the 21st. Grant met with President Lincoln and left for the front on the 24th.

Beginning in March, Sherman was gathering needed supplies and confiscating stores, wagons, and cattle from the citizens of Tennessee. President Lincoln wired Sherman that he had been informed, "Some of the poor Union people of Tennessee were left with nothing and you 'Sherman' should modify the orders of confiscation." Sherman answered Lincoln, "To provide for the necessities of the army, one or the other must quit and we cannot until the army of Joseph Johnston is conquered." Lincoln acquiesced. During their voyage, Sherman explained to Grant, his war strategy would be "Total War" on the Confederate Army and civilians alike. "Every day, every Rebel soldier's thought will be, that where I have been, their wives and families will be left with neither food nor shelter."

However, life in Wheeling continued on. Advertisements in the *Daily Intelligencer* during March included: "March 9 and 10, at Washington Hall, General Tom Thumb and his little wife, Lavinia Warren, the fascinating Queen of Beauty." "The St. Patrick's Mutual Relief Society will celebrate the 17th, by a parade in the afternoon. In the evening, there will be a lecture at the Cathedral." Subject: "The Illustrious Apostle of Ireland."

General Ulysses S. Grant passed through Wheeling several times without fanfare, traveling on Ohio River boats to connect to B&O railroad trains. *(Library of Congress)*

April 1864
By Bekah Karelis

The beginning of the month of April 1864 saw local citizens engaging in speculation of "condemned horses," offered for sale by the government. One hundred sixteen horses were quickly sold – some with plans to fatten them up and sell them back to the government, others, to simply resell to local citizens. For days, it was noted that these horses could be seen throughout the streets of Wheeling – a sad looking lot.

Around town, hefty criticism was given to the condition of the nation's flags flying on Market Street. First listed was the flag flying over the McLure House, described as "only equaled in raggedness, filthiness and all that is unseemly by the tattered and torn rag which floats at the mast head from Washington Hall." The flag at Washington Hall was as bad, if not worse, with its stars and stripes torn to shreds. Authorities at both establishments were berated by the newspaper for the sorry state of their nation's insignia.

It was at about this time that the government began looking to Wheeling for the establishment of a post hospital due to the city's location and accessibility. A hospital had been run out of the Athenaeum but had quickly filled. The Sanitary Commission supplied the soldiers with quilts, sheets, pillows, and other comforts in order to ease their suffering, but soldiers were still dying. Early April saw an outbreak of measles within its walls, killing several soldiers like Joseph Whiteman Phillips and Charles Cocherill. Both were from other areas of West Virginia but were buried in the Peninsula Cemetery.

The Soldier's Aid Society removed 45 of the patients from the Athenaeum to the Catholic hospital in North Wheeling at the end of March, and by April they were searching for a new location. At one point, the Houston house on Fourth Street (now Chapline) was considered, and then the south wing of the Catholic Hospital in North Wheeling (known today as Wheeling Hospital). Its location was more logical in terms of location and size.

Dr. John Kirker, who had been in charge of the Grafton Hospital, came to Wheeling on April 7 to take charge of the new post hospital. By the end of April, the decision was made. The post hospital was to be permanently run out of a wing in the Catholic Hospital. On April 29, $1000 worth of goods were transferred to the Catholic Hospital by a Mr. Price, a member of the Sanitary Commission for the City of Wheeling. A similar donation had been made to the Sanitary Commission through J. Marshall Hagans of Morgantown for the sum of $63.40. This was the first such donation that would be made toward the care of sick and incapacitated soldiers housed there.

After the country's experience with the horrific battles of Gettysburg and the bloody campaigns that followed, the government was having trouble finding the ability to responsibly care for the sick and wounded soldiers. The spring of 1864 was no different. After the Wilderness campaign and several disastrous conflicts elsewhere, Wheeling's post hospital filled to capacity in a very short time. By summer, the entire hospital was taken over and made ready for soldiers.

The month of April saw another interesting incident that was sensationalized by local newspapers. Referred to as the "Dusky Briggs Affair," it involved a local widow and a confederate soldier imprisoned in Wheeling. This young man, George Dusky, a notorious Confederate and son of an infamous bushwhacker, had been imprisoned in Wheeling earlier in the year after having been captured in Braxton County. This was not the first time Dusky had spent time in jail in Wheeling, having escaped after feigning an illness, being moved to the Spriggs Hospital, and managing to smuggle himself out a window. He was known as an "enterprising cutthroat."

A certain widow, Mollie Briggs, had somehow managed to make an acquaintance with this nefarious fellow and formed a strong attachment to him. She would visit with him and bring him packages to help ease his time in prison. After one incident, when she had attempted to smuggle contraband to him, she was banned from coming to his aid again. This did not deter the widow.

One evening at about 10 o'clock, a guardsman heard a suspicious sound outside one of the prison walls and went to investigate by candlelight. It was there that he found Ms. Briggs with a ladder and pole, trying to ease a package through an outside window into Mr. Dusky's prison cell. The guardsman attempted to seize Mrs. Briggs, who fell to the ground with the package spilling and spraying them both with nitric acid, seriously burning them both. To top it off, Ms. Briggs broke her leg above the knee. Later released under bail, the poor widow suffered for many months with her broken bone and burns, and it is unknown whatever became of their love affair. She did earn the title of an "uncompromising rebel."

In other news around town, a certain man learned that it was unwise to gallop quite so fast. Moses Hughes, guilty of galloping his horse across the Suspension Bridge and through the streets of the Island, was detained and arrested by Officer Richardson. He was taken before Alderman Robertson and fined $11.00! The newspaper commented, "Fast riding has become a very costly exercise."

Speaking of arrests: One of the editors of the *Intelligencer*, though not named, had the uncomfortable experience of being notified that he should consider himself under arrest by Major General Franz Sigel. It seemed that earlier in the year, the editor had published a letter that was considered contraband of war. Thankfully, it took only a few quick telegrams and some explanation to clear the matter up, and he was acquitted of all charges.

Quite ironically, a soldier by the name of "Jeff Davis" was arrested in North Wheeling for disorderly conduct. And there was yet another attempted escape from the Athenaeum, also known as Abraham Lincoln's Bastille. This particular prisoner, housed on the second floor of the building, cut a hole in the floor about 12 inches square and quietly as he could, dropped through to the floor below. The room below was dark, and unbeknownst to him, a sleeping soldier lay directly beneath the hole he had cut. His efforts to escape earned him a new home in the "Bastille" – this time in a four-by-six foot cell.

This Wheeling Hospital building dates from 1856, when the hospital moved from Fifteenth Street. It was staffed by Sisters of St. Joseph, six of whom, with Mother de Chantal Keating in charge, were eventually enrolled as U. S. Army nurses. In the spring of 1864, increasing casualties resulted in many patients being sent to Wheeling and other locations farther from the battlefields. *(Diocese of Wheeling Charleston Archives)*

May 1864

By Jeanne Finstein

May of 1864 was quite eventful for many Wheeling soldiers who were involved in the Battle of New Market in eastern Virginia. Although not considered a major battle of the war, it was significant for Wheeling because both the 1st West Virginia Infantry and Carlin's Battery were involved. This battle also included the cadet corps of the Virginia Military Institute, which had an infantry battalion of 247 cadets and a two-gun artillery section. The battle was part of Gen. Ulysses S. Grant's strategy to control the strategically important and agriculturally rich Shenandoah Valley. Union forces were led by Major General Franz Sigel; Major General John C. Breckinridge led the Confederates. The May 15 battle was a Confederate victory, and Union General Sigel was subsequently removed from his command.

A report written by one of the members of Carlin's Battery described some of the events. "On the evening of the 14th we heard brisk cannonading towards New Market. That night we got orders to march. At 4 o'clock, a.m. we could see the smoke of the artillery; waited about half an hour, and got orders to go to the front. The enemy was pushing Sigel hard. ...Our lines were giving way; we awaited the rebels approach; for a few moments all firing ceased; then we heard a loud shout, and we knew they were coming; soon they made their appearance in long black lines. We opened at good range, but on they came as if on dress parade; shell and canister flew through them, but on they came.

"I cannot describe to you the scene, but it was awful; ten pieces pouring canister into them at one hundred fifty yards and not moving them... The First [West] Virginia is the only regiment that charged; they alone could do nothing but fall, which many of them did. We [Carlin's Battery] were ordered to limber to the rear, but before we could do so the rebel line in front of us raised and killed two horses on one of our pieces. Before we could get new horses they were too close, and we were compelled to lighten and leave it... We then started, and down went three horses in our other piece. On they came, and this had to be abandoned, and down went three men who belonged to it: Geo. Bottles, a man from the Belmont Mills, shot through the left breast; Dan Morrison, shot through the body...W. Johnson fell here, and was run over with a gun, but the ground was soft, and he was not badly hurt."

A letter written to the *Daily Intelligencer* three days after the battle stated, "Major E[dward] W. Stephens commanded our Regiment and to his coolness, caution and military skill is owing to a great extent the success of the day's operations. In the hand of a less capable man all would have been lost...Our color Sergt., Wm. M. Ross, of Co. "C," carried the old flag through the battle, and although the banner is riddled and torn with shot and shell, not a bullet touched the bearer." Col. Joseph Thoburn was also praised for his action.

The Confederates lost 531 men, including ten of the VMI cadets killed in action. Union casualties were heavy, with a reported 841 killed, wounded, or missing. At least nine members of the First West Virginia Infantry and four from Carlin's Battery died. Listed among those wounded was William Stone, nephew of Wheeling's E.J. Stone (co-founder of the Stone and Thomas store). Wheeling's Benjamin Exley was a Corporal in Carlin's Battery at the time and presumably took part in the battle, escaping death, injury, and capture.

Among those killed was Martin Van Buren Manners, son of Wheeling's wharf master, Joseph Manners. When the 1st West Virginia Infantry withdrew, Martin's brother, Alexander Manners, remained with his wounded comrades and was captured by the Confederates. His fellow infantryman Henry C. Foster was also captured. Both men were sent to the infamous Andersonville Prison, where they languished under horrific conditions until their release nearly a year later on April 5, 1865. And both boarded the ill-fated *Sultana* steamer, headed back north to family and friends as the war was drawing to a close. The boiler of the overloaded *Sultana* exploded on the Mississippi River in the early morning hours of

April 27, 1865. Some 1700 men, women, and children died, making the disaster the worst in U.S. maritime history – with even more loss of life than the *Titanic*. Alexander Manners, who survived the battlefield and Andersonville Prison, was one of the casualties.

Henry Foster made it back to Wheeling. When the war had begun, the former brick maker enlisted in Company H of the 1st [West] Virginia Infantry, organized for three months. When that enlistment ended, he joined Company A of the newly organized 1st Infantry and served until his capture at New Market and subsequent imprisonment at Andersonville. After being released from the prison at the end of the war, he boarded the *Sultana* and headed for home. He was thrown into the water by the explosion and was rescued five hours later, while clinging to a tree. Back in Wheeling he resumed his former career as brick maker and later worked as a carpenter. In his application for a pension based on his service, he stated that he suffered from scurvy while at Andersonville "from want of food and from exposure." He also reported "debility or weakness of the whole system" from his experience in the water following the *Sultana* explosion. His pension application, however, was denied. He continued living in Wheeling until his death from pneumonia in 1890. He is buried in Mt. Wood Cemetery.

On a much lighter note, the *Daily Intelligencer* of May 23, 1864, reported the following. "Yesterday morning as a lot of exchanged prisoners were leaving the Baltimore and Ohio railroad depot to join their regiments, a woman, who to say the least of her, was no better than she should be, wept very bitterly and made some piteous appeals to be allowed to accompany one of the boys, who she said was her husband. Instead of being allowed to get aboard the train, she was committed to the Athenaeum, the soldier whom she claimed as her husband gladly assenting to the arrangement."

Although records indicated that Andersonville and *Sultana* survivor Henry Foster had been buried in Mt. Wood Cemetery, no monument marked his grave. Hiram Bowen of Barnesville, Ohio, installed a new marker at the cemetery, in honor of Foster's service. *(Photo by Jeanne Finstein)*

June 1864

By Robert DeFrancis

The pages of the *Daily Intelligencer* in Wheeling were virtually silent in June of 1864 about the first birthday of the new state of West Virginia. June 20 was not proclaimed to be of much importance, it seemed, being overshadowed by two major events that occurred in the city of Wheeling just before and slightly after that date. Of course, the Civil War was still being fought, and the newspapers that month were full of reports from the field, obituary announcements of the fallen, and official gubernatorial proclamations naming dozens of persons as enemies of the state.

Editors Archibald Campbell and John McDermot dutifully pushed Abraham Lincoln and Andrew Johnson for President and Vice President as their newspaper covered the national union (Republican) nominations at the Baltimore Convention June 7 and 8. As well, Campbell that month gave an early endorsement to the state's first governor, Arthur I. Boreman, to be renominated at the State Convention in August.

Despite the somber war dispatches, the newspapers in June 1864 were dominated by reports and advertisements for upcoming entertainments, one billed as the largest exhibition in the world, and the other an unprecedented charitable undertaking that came to be called "the Wheeling Sanitary Fair."

Imagine the excitement in town when a full two columns of newspaper space, top to bottom, were filled with details about Thayer & Noyes' United States Circus and Van Amburgh & Co.'s Mammoth Menagerie and Egyptian Caravan. "Combined for the Season of 1864, with One Price Admission. The Wonders of Animated Nature Consolidated with the only Legitimate Circus ever organized – Moral and Refined Amusement." This exciting exhibition would be on Wheeling Island Saturday, June 18, for two shows: 2 and 7 p.m. Admission was 50 cents for adults and 25 cents for children under 12. And just who, or what, would be there? The ad stipulated the following: "equestrians, acrobats, gymnasts, jesters, clowns, contortionists, equilibrists and general performers.

Trained horses, ponies and mules; lions, tigers, leopards, bears, hyenas, wolves, monkeys, baboons, and birds of all kinds."

But wait: that constituted just the small print. Reserved for the ad's major headlines was "the mammoth War Elephant Hannibal, the largest animal in the world, weighing nearly 1,600 pounds." Also to be seen: a hippopotamus, a white polar bear, an African ostrich, snow white peacocks and Japanese Maskin Swine, the first ever imported to America. "For the special amusement of Ladies and Children," Mr. Noyes "will exhibit his great performing monkey, Victor." A famed brass band drawn by 12 Arabian steeds would lead a "cavalcade, a moving panorama of over a mile in length."

The advertisement in question would be repeated at least a half-dozen times in various locations of several newspaper editions, quite a moneymaker for the *Daily Intelligencer*. Clearly, though, as always, advertising works. This is what the *Intelligencer* had to say about the event in the June 20 edition: "The parade of the Circus and Menagerie on Saturday, through the principal streets, was a great event for the rising generation. The streets and sidewalks were crowded with children, many of whom crowded in dangerous proximity to the large elephant Hannibal, lifting up his gold foiled covering and dancing in great joy about his immense pins. A terrible dust was kicked up by the wagons, horses and mules and the town was startled from its propriety for about an hour."

Elsewhere in the same edition, it was reported, "Thayer & Noyes' Circus and Menagerie exhibited on the Island Saturday afternoon and evening. Never did we see such a crowd as assembled underneath the pavilion on Saturday afternoon. There were not less than five thousand persons, men, women and children of all colors and conditions, and babies in arms by the hundred.

"The afternoon was intensely hot, and the sun poured down with great fierceness upon the great tent full of humanity, which soon turned as red as the 'snout' of a turkey gobbler, and muslin and linen garments were completely saturated with perspiration.

The peddlers of circus water (lemonade) were yelling, and the babies and the monkeys squealing and crying. The people crowded about the ring so that there was great delay in getting ready for the performance. Several persons fainted, and all who could force a passage through the crowd left before the performance had fairly commenced. In the evening the crowd was not so great, and the exhibition was witnessed with more satisfaction."

Another event apparently had preoccupied Wheeling residents for weeks before the appearance of the circus and menagerie. The *Daily Intelligencer* on June 8 reported, "The patriotic citizens of Wheeling, determined not to be behind other cities in the great work of furnishing means for the benefit of the Sanitary and Christian Commissions, are making extensive preparations for holding a fair to be opened on the 28th ..."

The United States Sanitary Commission was a private relief agency created by federal legislation on June 18, 1861, to support sick and wounded soldiers of the U.S. Army during the Civil War. It operated across the North and raised an estimated $25 million in revenue and in-kind contributions to support the cause. Thousands volunteered. The first Sanitary Fair was held in Chicago from October 27-November 7, 1863.

The *Daily Intelligencer* columns trumpeted Wheeling's event thusly, "Grand Patriotic Festival and Fair, on behalf of the Sanitary Commission, Christian Commission, and Soldiers' Aid Societies, to be held in the Fair Buildings, commencing June 28, 1864, and continuing for one week, including a Grand Celebration on the Fourth of July."

Throughout the month, the newspaper reported in detail on the names of individuals and groups that donated money to the Sanitary Fair. Special pleas were extended for help from "farmers, manufacturers, mechanics and workingmen, merchants, ladies, ministers of the gospel, citizens of neighboring towns and children" who were urged to, "Save your pocket money and spend it at the

Patriotic Festival. There it will bring you all it is worth and heal many a wound beside." At the fair, one could buy refreshments, bouquets and useful and fancy articles. On the stage to be erected would be "recherché amusements and entertainments of various kinds" each evening. Special pleas were made for donation of items to be displayed in the "Curiosity Shop and Gallery of Fine Arts."

On June 25 the newspaper reminded its readers "there remains but little time" to donate to the fair. "Nearly all of our people here are giving liberally of their means and their time. Indeed the fair has become the absorbing business of the city." In the June 30 edition, the *Intelligencer* reported, "the sale of tickets was quite as good as was anticipated" for the opening day.

Highlights of the event included the Grand Bazaar where fairgoers could see, and perhaps buy, just about any item they might need, from socks to cutlery to toy horses for the children. There were exhibitions by glassblowers, and the newspaper pointed out, "A printing press from this office was in operation and attracted some attention from those unfamiliar with the black art." On display was a nail machine "worked by Master William Beymer, a mere child, whose father was recently killed in the service of his country."

Apparently, many of the more unique items donated were the subject of raffles, with chances being sold by young ladies overseeing the booths. Voluminous details were reported on the fair buildings, including the dining hall and the floral hall, which contained a French garden scene, complete with a house surrounded by woods, flowers, grass, shrubbery, and fountains.

The *USS Monitor* was an iron-hulled steamship built during the Civil War, the first ironclad warship commissioned by the Union Navy. A replica, the *Little Monitor*, could be found in Monitor Hall, "on the opposite corner of the street from the Fair buildings, in the Athenaeum prison yard. Any and every single part of the model, multiplied by twenty-four, will produce the original *Monitor*." A canal was constructed in the hall to display the *Little Monitor*.

There was quite an historical artifact in the Gallery of Fine Arts and Curiosities: "an old cross cut saw, used for sawing the logs with which Fort Henry was built in 1777, where Wheeling now stands;" a bible printed in 1530, and General Washington's piano. However, a note of caution was made also. "We understand that there was a fresh arrival of pickpockets in the city yesterday. Persons visiting the fair will govern themselves accordingly."

In the Monday, July 4, edition of the newspaper, the editors took note that the decision was made to continue the fair for the entire week. "Everything goes swimmingly at the Fair. The result promises to exceed all original calculations. Saturday and Saturday night the halls were crowded and the receipts in all the departments are represented as large." But the editors received a letter with some suggestions to improve the fair and said, "We introduce them to our readers with our hearty endorsement." The correspondent urged merchants and shopkeepers to "close up business promptly and universally at 6 p.m." to allow their employees to attend the evening fair activities. More importantly, the writer discussed "the present price of admission. Very many of our citizens think it too high, and it is too high." The writer pointed out, "We are largely a community of the middle class...and if the price was put at one half the present rates, I think there is no doubt, but more money would be realized in the end."

Great Van Amburgh Himself;

WILL EXHIBIT AT WHEELING,
ON
WHEELING ISLAND,
ON
SATURDAY, JUNE 18th, 1864,

Doors open at 2 and 7 o'clock. P. M.
Admission 50c. Children under 12 years of age
25c.

THE MAMMOTH
WAR ELEPHANT HANNIBAL;

Circus entertainment helped Wheeling's citizens take their minds off war news. This ad promises a visit to Wheeling Island of the "Great Van Amburgh Himself" and the "Mammoth War Elephant Hannibal," among other oddities. *(Daily Intelligencer, June 1864)*

July 1864
By Charles A. Julian

Civil War events and skirmishes often provide interesting glimpses into little known local happenings – including how George Washington became a Civil War spoil ultimately landing in Wheeling, West Virginia. From June 10-14, 1864, Union General David Hunter occupied the Shenandoah Valley town of Lexington, Virginia, resulting in ruin and destruction. On June 12th Yankee troops burned nearby Virginia Military Institute (VMI), and Hunter's soldiers pulled down a locally-revered, life-size statue of George Washington as a spoil of war.

The VMI statue was a replica of Jean-Antoine Houdon's Washington statue featured prominently at Virginia State Capitol's Rotunda in Richmond. For eight years, Washington's iconic image stood unmolested in a place of honor on VMI's campus. Colonel David Hunter Strother (later known as Porte Crayon) convinced General Hunter to send the statue to Wheeling (instead of to the U.S. Military Institute at West Point) later observing, "the statue was a fine work of art standing naked and unprotected under the ruined walls of the Institute, liable to be crushed by their fall." Strother observed that, "as I looked at the dignified and noble countenance I felt indignant that this effigy should be left to adorn a country whose inhabitants were striving to destroy a government which he founded."

The captured statue was packed and loaded onto a wagon and later transferred to a Baltimore and Ohio railroad car for its trip to Wheeling. The statue arrived safely in Wheeling on July 2, 1864, although some Southerners were misinformed that it was broken into pieces and ruined because the enemy was unable to negotiate the mountain passes of Virginia.

At the time of the statue's arrival, a Sanitary Fair, designed to raise money for the care of sick soldiers and prisoners, was underway on Wheeling Island. Organizers of the Fair (which opened on June 28th) featured displays and other patriotic venues. The Washington statue was prominently displayed in the Fair's Great Hall, where it was promised by the local newspaper to be worth the price of admission. It remained on public display until the fair's closure on July 9th. However, not all parties endorsed the pilfering of the marble treasure. The *New York News* noted that the deed was "an act of vandalism without earthly excuse – it is a theft that nothing cannot palliate – disgraceful to the age, and doubly so to the country that will suffer such a sacrifice to go unwhipped of justice."

The *Daily Intelligencer* editor Archibald W. Campbell on July 4th wrote, "We must confess that we see nothing in the enterprise to commend. We could not feel like congratulating the Fair on Saturday on the possession of this trophy. The bringing of it away from Lexington was an act of vandalism that must be objectionable to all right thinking people, irrespective of their hatred for the rebels."

At the Sanitary Fair's conclusion, the statue was relocated from Wheeling Island to West Virginia's temporary capitol building grounds at Linsly Institute, where from July 1864 until just after the Civil War's conclusion in April 1865 it remained on public display. On October 14, 1865, David Hunter Strother, in his post-war capacity as Adjutant General of the Virginia Militia, wrote to West Virginia Governor Arthur I. Boreman recommending return of the statue. Boreman did not oppose its return but decided that the West Virginia Legislature should authorize its removal from Wheeling. The Legislature agreed.

On January 27, 1866, Wheeling *Daily Register* editors published Washington's Second Farewell Address full of satirical references and written from the anthropomorphic viewpoint of the statue. Passages harkening to the routing of VMI, wryly invoked "the warm, burning invitation of Major General Hunter..." a reference to the fires set by Hunter's men. Or, the reference to the statue's uprooting, "...and honored me with a floor of one of his army wagons" as well as witty asides like "...For myself, I felt too heavy at heart to stir," a reference to the statue's weight.

The statue noted, "...under these pleasant and fragrant circumstances, I arrived at the seat of your Capital, and was duly installed in my present unmerited and unsought position," no doubt a reference to the ignoble journey in the Army wagon.

In his Second Farewell Address, Washington (the statue) notes, "For more than eighteen months I have been a solitary sentinel at your Capitol. Your Governor has frequently passed and re-passed me without a word. I cannot feel at home here. I wish to return to that sacred spot from whence I was drafted by that heartless Hunter." The *Register* editors cheekily added, "But you must have noticed from the cast of my countenance and general frame that I have an iron constitution and you will remember that the age in which my composition was moulded has conduced to bronze my complexion, so that, those gentle and delicate lines of embrazonment, which usually illumine fair features, cannot now be traced in mine," all humorous references to statues and monuments.

The statuesque Washington concludes his address, "Therefore relying on the generosity of Governor Boreman and the legal wisdom of the Senator referred to, with a conscience, though hardened now, yet void of offence; in the hope of a speedy restoration of all my country, and of my place on the pedestal from which I was rudely torn, I bid you, all an affectionate farewell."

Upon completion of the necessary transportation logistics, Governor Boreman was presented with a receipt for "one bronze statue which was taken from the Virginia Military Institute by General Hunter during the late war."

On September 10, 1866, former Virginia Governor John Letcher (whose home was burned by Hunter's men) spoke for several hours at the statue's VMI Re-Inauguration ceremony. Thus, after a two-year absence, the statue of General George Washington (perhaps one of the Civil War's most improbable prisoners of war) was returned to its rightful site where it continues to be afforded a place of honor and respect from both Yankees and Rebels.

This life-size statue of George Washington was taken by Union soldiers from Virginia Military Institute and was sent to Wheeling as a spoil of war. After the war, it was returned. This photo shows cadets and townspeople in front of the statue at VMI in 1866. *(Courtesy of the Virginia Military Institute Archives)*

August 1864
Jeanne Finstein

The Shenandoah Campaign was undoubtedly on the minds of many Wheeling residents during the month of August 1864 as letters and newspaper reports relayed news from the locally based units that were involved in that area. The August 1 *Daily Intelligencer* reported that some twelve to fifteen hundred "of our brave sick and wounded soldiers" had been admitted to the Cumberland and Claryville, Maryland hospitals. Wheeling's George K. Wheat visited the hospitals and provided a list of dozens of area men who had been hospitalized, along with their units and the nature of their wounds or illnesses.

Among those mentioned in the paper and still being mourned was Col. Daniel Frost, a St. Clairsville native and former newspaper editor of the Virginia Chronicle in Ravenswood, WV. Frost was an ardent Union supporter and had been elected Speaker of the House of the Restored Government of Virginia. He was 43 years old when he enlisted, considered old for a recruit at that time. He served as colonel of the 11th West Virginia Infantry and had been mortally wounded on July 18 at the Battle of Snicker's Ferry (sometimes called the Battle of Cool Spring). His remains were returned to Wheeling's Mt. Wood Cemetery.

C.J. Rawling, a member of the 1st Infantry and author of the book that chronicles its activities, reported on the locations of that unit during the month. "On the 7th General [Philip] Sheridan took command of the army for operations in the Shenandoah Valley, and on the 8th of August the regiment again crossed the Potomac at Harper's Ferry, and bivouacked on the banks of the Shenandoah near Halltown. The regiment has camped on the banks of this stream many times during the past two and a half years, and its beautiful waters have become quite familiar to the men. How long will they be moved up and down the river is a question they put to each other, but none can answer it." The regiment marched up and down the valley during most of the month, seeing little action other than picket duty and a few skirmishes. Rawling reported that on the 18th the men "were now feasting on green corn and foraging for hogs, chickens, apples, etc., which, as may be supposed, were valuable and welcome additions to the marching ration."

Late in the month, the regiment found itself very near a Confederate unit. Rawling reported, "On the 25th the picket-firing was again very active, but towards the close of the day there was a cessation of firing, during which the men began to fraternize. 'Yank' and 'Johnny' conversed together, which led to an exchange of papers, tobacco, coffee, etc., then banterings and course jokes; finally hostilities were resumed, and the men that a little while ago were exchanging coffee and tobacco and the news were again exchanging leaden compliments – such was army life."

Thomas Jefferson Orr, a member of the 12th Infantry and author of numerous letters home to friends and relatives, seemed tired and hungry during this period. On August 5 he wrote to his parents from his post in the eastern panhandle, "The boys are beginning to get very tired of West Va. they would rather go to the army of the Potomack they feed them better there...I heard Giff Frazier and Eugean Dunlap say that they had picked beans for two hours out of horse dung on the road to get about a half tinful which they cooked and eat and was glad to get." Fortunately, a supply shipment arrived soon after the letter was written, including "onions pickels potatoes pork beef hard tack coffee sugar beans etc. which makes very good living."

Meanwhile, Battery D of the First West Virginia Light Artillery, better known as Carlin's Battery, spent the latter part of the month and the first half of September in Wheeling, recruiting additional men and receiving new guns. The *Intelligencer* reported that, "The men looked travel worn and weary enough, and are bronzed by the suns of Dixie; but we are glad to learn that all are in good health and spirits." The Battery was welcomed to Wheeling with a brass band, and "hundreds of people followed, and the wildest excitement prevailed for a time." The names of thirty-eight new recruits made the paper on August 23.

Efforts to meet the general recruitment quota, established after President Lincoln issued a call for an additional 500,000 men, were recorded throughout the month. A bounty of $310 (the equivalent of over $4500 today) was offered for every volunteer, plus $10 to the person presenting an acceptable recruit. Officials were confident that the quota would be met, asserting that, "Ohio County has never yet and never will allow a draft to take place within her limits." A few "professional bounty jumpers" were arrested during these recruitment efforts and confined to jail until it was time for them to be "shipped to the field." The paper stated that, "Bounty jumping will doubtless be continued until a little hanging and shooting is administered." By the early days of September, most or all counties in the northern panhandle had filled their quotas.

Some 360 Rebel prisoners arrived in Wheeling on August 11, including at least five who had left Wheeling to join the Confederate forces – Richard Stanberry, William Love, Samuel Voltz, Michael Sheckey, and Alexander Caldwell. The prisoners were housed temporarily in the Athenaeum, before being sent the next day to Camp Chase, in Columbus. The paper reported, "The whole gang of prisoners look exceedingly hard in the way of attire but they have a very healthy look in other respects. Some are without shoes, and hardly a man among the number has a whole suit of clothes. They all express a desire to be entered for exchange and refuse to take the oath."

The paper also reported that the local police had been "dealing very vigorously with the disreputable women who are in the habit of parading the streets of the city; in consequence of which many of them have donned male attire. Several of these women are now in the city dressed in men's clothing."

Prices were listed for items at the Second Ward market, in preparation for the national day of thanksgiving scheduled for August 5: corn, 25 cents a dozen; tomatoes $2 a peck; potatoes 80 cents a peck; and cucumbers 60 cents a dozen. "Green peas and all sorts of berries, except blackberries, are out of season and of course cannot be had at any price." The actual day of thanksgiving, a Thursday, "saw the city as quiet as upon a Sabbath day, and no business whatever was done. Services were held in the churches, all of which were tolerably well attended. Hundreds of people went to picnics in the country, and there was scarcely a vehicle or a beast of burden left in town."

On August 21, the cornerstone was laid for the new Academy and Convent of the Sisters of Visitation near the city. A long, front-page article described the planned "massive" structure – later known as Mt. De Chantal. The article boasts that the structure would feature low-pressure steam heat, gas manufactured on-site for lighting, and "all the conveniences found in the most finished private residences." Cars on the Hempfield Railroad reportedly carried "several thousand" people to the celebration. This building stood nearly 150 years before being demolished.

The cornerstone of Mount de Chantal Visitation Academy was laid in August 1864. This early photo shows the school under construction. The school itself was begun in downtown Wheeling in 1848, predating both the formation of the state of West Virginia and the establishment of the Diocese of Wheeling. The school served generations of students until it closed in 2008. Demolition of this structure began in late 2011. *(Diocese of Wheeling-Charleston Archives)*

September 1864
By Joseph Laker

Wheeling's two newspapers, the *Daily Intelligencer* and the *Daily Register* offered their readers competing interpretations and answers for the national and state problems in September 1864. The *Intelligencer*, published by Archibald Campbell and John McDermot, favored the Union, the Republican Party, the Lincoln administration, and West Virginia's separation from Virginia. The *Register*, published by Lewis Baker and O. S. Long, supported the Democratic Party, frequently criticized Lincoln, and favored a more conciliatory policy toward the Confederacy.

As the national and state electioneering in 1864 heated up, the *Intelligencer* daily published the slate of the Union (Republican) national, state, and local ticket and printed many articles critical of the Democratic platform and its presidential and vice-presidential candidates, General George McClellan and Senator George Pendleton of Ohio. The *Register*, on the other hand, daily printed the Democratic ticket, praised its nominees, and claimed "Abraham Lincoln is striving by the exercise of force and bribery and fraud to perpetuate and strengthen his power over the lives and liberties of the people." The *Register* claimed Lincoln was responsible for the deaths of Union soldiers in Confederate prisons because he refused Confederate requests to exchange prisoners. It accused Lincoln's government of buying army supplies when prices were highest in order to "fill the coffers of contractors and shoddy men who were in the pay and interest of the administration."

Both newspapers carried out election polling on trains, at train stations, and among soldiers, but their results showed opposite results. People polled by the *Intelligencer* overwhelmingly favored Lincoln; those surveyed by the *Daily Register* strongly preferred McClellan.

After being suppressed by the army for more than two months, the *Register* resumed publication on September 22nd with a long story about the paper's suspension. At 3:00 p.m. on July 9th, Captain Ewald Over with three armed Union soldiers showed up at the *Register*'s building and arrested the newspaper's editors,

Baker and Long, and put them in the Athenaeum. An armed soldier was placed at the door to prevent entrance; employees were
forced to leave. Captain Over acted on orders sent by General David
Hunter. No charges were filed against the editors, and their letters
to Generals Hunter, George Crook, and Benjamin F. Kelley asking
for an explanation were ignored until after General Hunter was
dismissed from his command. Hunter's replacement, General Philip
Sheridan, ordered the editors to be released on August 30th. Once
freed the editors learned that while the *Register*'s office was closed
and under armed guard, their private papers had been searched
and destroyed. In addition, type was ruined and printing materials
were stolen. The *Register*'s editors speculated that Hunter had
suppressed the newspaper because of the *Register*'s criticism of
Hunter's military tactics against the Confederates at Lynchburg.
And because the *Register* was the only Democratic paper in West
Virginia, some abolitionists wanted the paper destroyed. They
claimed their rights were arbitrarily denied by Hunter, "a commander whose only military exploits have been the plundering of
defenseless towns and the murder of unarmed citizens."

During September Union armies and navy made significant
gains against the Confederates, which helped ensure Lincoln's
election to a second term in November. Sheridan won a series of
battles against the rebel forces in the Shenandoah Valley and by
the end of the month had begun to destroy the food supplies there
that were so vital to the Confederacy. On the first of September Gen.
William Sherman seized Atlanta, soon forced all civilians from the
city, and then destroyed it by fire. He then began his destructive
march to the coast to eliminate rebel resources. While not achieving
a decisive breakthrough, Generals Ulysses S. Grant and George
Meade advanced against Confederate forces defending Richmond
forcing the rebels to extend their defensive lines. The Union navy
tightened its blockade of the South and closed its two important
ports, Mobile, Alabama, and Charleston, South Carolina.

The Confederacy responded by launching offenses in Tennessee and Missouri to force the Union armies to abandon their strategies in the East, but by the end of the month these attacks had petered out. On September 18th a band of 34 Confederate rebels seized two steamboats on lake Erie as part of a plot to seize the federal warship *U. S. Michigan*. With control of the *Michigan*, they planned to attack the federal prison on Johnson's Island to free the some 5,000 rebels held there. The plot, which was eerily similar to one attempted in September 1863, also failed, and many of the plotters were captured.

Wheeling was racked by violence during much of September. The police struck for higher wages, and while one chamber of the city council agreed to raise salaries, the other chamber refused. Citizens demanded a tripling of the number of police. At one point only one officer was on active duty, and the army briefly took over the job of maintaining order. Among the violence facing the citizens were a foiled attempt by Confederate prisoners to escape by tunnel from the Athenaeum, and the beating and robbery of a number of soldiers who had received bounties to enlist in the army. The most controversial shooting incident occurred on September 19th when three policemen shot Isaac Harris in the face, shoulder, and groin in the Second Ward market house. Earlier in the day officers Sautmires and Scroggins had attempted to arrest Harris on misdemeanor charges, but Harris and a friend resisted and fled the scene. Harris went home, drank some beer, and returned to the market with an axe handle threatening to kill the officers. Harris struck both officers who fled into the market house. When Harris followed, he was shot. A grand jury exonerated the officers several weeks later.

The *Intelligencer* reported on the 17th that rebel prisoners in the Athenaeum were catching, cooking, and eating rats due to limited rations. Captain Over investigated and found that some young men, not due to short rations but curiosity, were eating rats, which they claimed tasted like squirrel. Over gave the men permission to continue to do so.

As editor and part owner of Wheeling's *Daily Intelligencer* newspaper, Archibald W. Campbell was in a powerful position to be a leader in the statehood movements. He had graduated in 1852 from Bethany College, an institution founded by his uncle, Alexander Campbell, and soon entered the newspaper business. His strong editorials favored the new Republican Party, the abolishment of slavery, and the preservation of the Union. It is said that a telegram written by him to President Lincoln convinced the President to sign the West Virginia statehood bill. *(Wheeling Hall of Fame)*

October 1864

By Kate Quinn

In October 1864 the local newspapers were full of reports of political conventions as election day drew closer. Many soldiers were allowed to return home to vote, and Wheeling held one political meeting after another with torch light parades for President Lincoln and rallies with Waitman Willey as the speaker for McClellan. "Little Napolean," as McClelland was nicknamed, wanted the war to stop immediately and called for negotiations with the Rebels.

Major Kelley reported that women and children were robbed of their clothing by Rebel soldiers in Braxton County. Fashion dictated that men should not wear white shirts; Baltimore boots were all the rage; and women were advised to hitch up their skirts "so as not to clean the streets." Battles raged on in the Shenandoah Valley with General William Sherman in the lead.

By October 20 news had reached Wheeling of the death in battle of Col. Joseph Thoburn, a dearly loved surgeon from Wheeling. Thoburn was born in County Antrim, Ireland, and his family came to America where he grew up near St. Clairsville, Ohio. He studied medicine and eventually became a doctor in Wheeling. When war broke out in 1861 he enlisted and became the surgeon for the First [West] Virginia Infantry. The men chose him as their colonel when they later enlisted for three-year service. Thoburn was present when Colonel Benjamin Franklin Kelley, the first officer wounded in the war, was shot in Philippi and accompanied him back to Wheeling for treatment.

In 1862, Thoburn led the First Virginia in a charge against Stonewall Jackson's forces at the First Battle of Kernstown. With his hat on the tip of his sword, Thoburn lead his men forward, but went down wounded as his troops fought fellow Virginians. He recovered in time to lead his regiment again at the Battle of Port Republic. That summer he participated in the campaign in Northern Virginia under Gen. John Pope as a brigade commander at Cedar Mountain and Second Manassas. In the fall he served as a regimental and brigade commander guarding the B & O railroad and chasing down Rebel raiders throughout West Virginia for eighteen months.

In the spring of 1864, Thoburn returned to the Shenandoah Valley as a brigade commander. His troops covered the retreat of the defeated Union soldiers at New Market. He met his fate at the Battle of Cedar Creek as he attempted to rally the troops, shot by a Rebel soldier wearing the uniform of the North and dying on the streets of Middletown. Known to his troops as "Cool Joe," Thoburn was beloved by his men, and General George Crook wrote of him, "I am pained to report the death of Col. Joseph Thoburn, commanding First Division, and Capt. Phillip G. Bier, assistant adjutant-general on my staff. Both fell mortally wounded while rallying the men. Brave, efficient, and ever conspicuous for their gallantry on the field of battle in them the country sustained a loss not easily repaired".

A large crowd greeted the train as the remains were brought to Wheeling in a plain wooden coffin. The body, which had been covered in boxwood, a sign of friendship and farewell, was properly dressed and placed in a metal coffin at the depot. The remains were then taken by hearse to the home of Thoburn's brother-in-law, Mr. James Wilson of Center Wheeling. Friends and family came by the residence for a last glimpse of their loved one.

A committee of the Central Union Club, which included Mayor Henry Crangle, planned the funeral service. The bodies of Thoburn, Bier, and Sergeant Benjamin Jenkins of the 1st West Virginia Calvary were to lie in state in the State House for two days. Funeral services were held at the Fourth Street M.E. Church, followed by a procession to Mt. Wood cemetery. Capt. John McLure had generously donated enough ground to bury sixty to seventy soldiers and hoped that the land would be consecrated for all who were buried there.

As the procession formed, flags flew at half-mast, and the city was draped in mourning attire. All businesses were closed. The coffins were taken from the Capitol to the M.E church and placed on the altar. The huge crowd could not fit into the church so hundreds stood outside. General Benjamin Kelley served as one of the pallbearers. The procession up Market Street to Mt. Wood saw hundreds lining the streets, as the largest funeral the city had ever seen passed by. At the cemetery, again a huge crowd watched as three volleys were fired over each of the three heroes' graves.

Irish immigrant Dr. Joseph Thoburn was commissioned as surgeon of the First [West] Virginia regiment, under Col. Benjamin F. Kelley, in the three months' service. He attended the wounded Kelley at the Battle of Philippi. Following the end of the first three months of the war, he was commissioned colonel of the First [West] Virginia Infantry and led his regiment in the numerous battles, until he was killed in the Battle of Cedar Creek on October 19, 1864. *(From the collection of Linda Fluharty)*

November 1864
By Jeanne Finstein

Civil War activities for Wheeling-based military units in November 1864 were relatively light. As General William Tecumseh Sherman left Atlanta to begin his legendary "march to the sea," many of the men in the First West Virginia Infantry returned home, their three-year enlistment period having ended. About 250 of the men re-enlisted in the First and remained in the Cumberland, Maryland, area, later consolidating with the re-enlisted men of the Fourth West Virginia. The Twelfth West Virginia Infantry spent most of the month near Winchester, Virginia, and Carlin's Battery was stationed in Parkersburg.

Much of the news in the early part of the month focused on the presidential election, with Abraham Lincoln facing General George B. McClellan on November 8. Throughout the summer, Lincoln had feared that he would lose the election. The country had not elected an incumbent President for a second term since Andrew Jackson had defeated Henry Clay in 1832 — nine Presidents in a row had served just one term. Also, Lincoln's embrace of emancipation was a problem for many Northern voters, and he had staunch opponents in Congress. But worst of all, the war had not been going well.

On August 23 Lincoln had called his cabinet together and asked them to sign the back of a sealed document. The document was a memorandum that stated, "This morning, as for some days past, it seems exceedingly probably that this Administration will not be re-elected. Then it will be my duty to so co-operate with the President-elect, as to save the Union between the election and the inauguration; as he will have secured his election on such ground that he can not possibly save it afterwards."

Everything changed, however, in early September 1864 when General Sherman seized Atlanta. The war effort had turned decidedly in the North's favor, making Lincoln's re-election much more likely. His party's platform called for pursuit of the war until the Confederacy surrendered unconditionally, a constitutional amendment for the abolition of slavery, aid to disabled Union veterans, continued

European neutrality, enforcement of the Monroe Doctrine, encouragement of immigration, and construction of a transcontinental railroad. Andrew Johnson, former Senator and current Military Governor of Tennessee, was Lincoln's running mate.

Meanwhile, the Democratic Party was bitterly split between War Democrats and Peace Democrats, who further divided among competing factions. After the Battle of Gettysburg, when it was clear the South could no longer win the war, moderate Peace Democrats proposed a negotiated peace that would secure Union victory without devastating the South. Radical Peace Democrats, known as Copperheads, declared the war to be a failure and favored an immediate end to hostilities without securing Union victory.

In an attempt to unify the party that was divided by issues of war and peace, the Democrats compromised by selecting pro-war General George B. McClellan for President and anti-war George H. Pendleton for Vice-President. The Democrats then adopted a peace platform — a platform that McClellan personally rejected. A tongue-in-cheek report stated that McClellan, criticized throughout the war for being slow to attack, would never be inaugurated if he should happen to be elected, because he would never be ready.

With the central issue of the election being the war, the question of absentee voting for soldiers arose. The presidential candidates offered two distinct choices for the soldiers: a vote for Lincoln meant the continuation of the war; a vote for McClellan offered the immediate end of hostilities and the possibility of returning home quickly. It might seem that the soldiers would rather vote to end the war so they could return home, but a vote for McClellan would invalidate the sacrifices that they and their comrades had made. As one soldier put it, "I can not vote for one thing and fight for another."

By the time of the November 1864 general election, the Union Army consisted of approximately one million men in uniform, most of whom were stationed outside their home state. The Navy added another 59,000, nearly all of whom were assigned to ships at sea. During prior elections, soldiers had been furloughed and traveled home to cast their ballots. But with such a large number of men away from home in 1864, absentee balloting became a hot issue.

Steps had been taken by most states to ensure that their soldiers in the field could vote. Some states permitted soldiers to vote by proxy, with vote choices sent home to an individual who would cast votes on the soldier's behalf. Wheeling's *Daily Intelligencer* reported that on October 31 the "soldier's friend," Jacob Hornbrook, arrived in Wheeling, "suffering from fatigue and exhaustion" but bringing some 1500 soldiers' votes. A group of 115 men from the Second West Virginia Cavalry arrived in Wheeling the day before the election, and 103 of them stated that they supported Lincoln and Johnson, with the other 12 saying that they "are for fighting as they have done for over three years, until the Union is established and traitors, home and abroad, have learned to obey the laws of the land."

Nationwide, only about 150,000 soldiers were able to cast absentee ballots from the field, but the soldier vote proved crucial to re-electing President Lincoln. From the twelve states allowing absentee voting for military personnel, tallies show that 78% of these men voted for Lincoln.

With the help of the soldiers' ballots, Lincoln won by more than 400,000 popular votes. The electoral count was more impressive, with Lincoln winning 212 to 21. Only three states that had remained in the Union – New Jersey, Delaware, and Kentucky – cast their electoral votes for McClellan.

The total West Virginia count was 23,799 (68%) for Lincoln and 11,078 (32%) for McClellan. Although the pro-Lincoln *Intelligencer* had been very vocal in his support, the Lincoln margin of victory in Ohio County was surprisingly small: Lincoln 2139 and McClellan 2008. However, Lincoln's victory was celebrated with gusto by the workers at LaBelle Nail, who fired 35 rounds from their old "baby waker" – the "Garibaldi" cannon.

President Lincoln interpreted his re-election as a mandate that the war should continue until the country was reunified, without slavery. Historians point out the importance of the 1864 election, when Lincoln could have made a case to retain his presidency without an election because of the war. The fact that the democratic process continued unimpaired was a testimony to the American democratic system of government.

Throughout the war years and before, the building now known as West Virginia Independence Hall stood on the corner of Market and 16th Streets. Election celebrations undoubtedly took place here. The building never served as the capitol of the state but housed the Restored Government of Virginia from 1861-1863. The image shows what the "Custom House" looked like during that time. *(Ohio County Public Library Archives)*

December 1864

By David Javersak

Arthur I. Boreman became West Virginia's first governor on June 20, 1863. His portrait, from the early years of the Civil War, shows a man of stern countenance, deeply-set eyes, clenched mouth, and full beard. His demeanor is serious and determined, befitting the man at the center of the drama that created the 35th state. Born in Waynesburg, Pennsylvania, in 1823, he came to Middlebourne, Tyler County, as a toddler. After an education at the local school, he studied law with an older brother and brother-in-law. In the mid-1840s, he relocated to Parkersburg, a city he called home until his death. As a Whig, he had won election to the Virginia Legislature in 1855 and held that office until April 1861, when he left Richmond to return to Wood County to oppose Virginia's secession.

In June, he travelled to Wheeling as a member of the Second Wheeling Convention; his colleagues selected him as their presiding officer. That convention established the Restored State of Virginia and approved the formation of West Virginia. Securing the nomination of the Constitutional Union Party, he ran for and easily won the contest for governor in the spring of 1863. During the first two of his three terms, his administration faced problems of every sort: lack of money, disloyal citizens, uncooperative county governments, on-going military conflicts within state borders, and difficulties inherent in creating a new political infrastructure. Yet, somehow amidst all this turmoil and tumult, he found time to fall in love and marry,

Four weeks after his re-election on November 2, 1864, he took a wife; he was 41 years old. The Civil War brought him to Wheeling, and the Civil War made possible his union with Lauranne Tanner Bullock. The couple exchanged their vows at the Fourth Street Methodist Church with the Rev. Alexander Martin as officiant. Three years later, during Boreman's third term, Martin became West Virginia University's first president.

The new Mrs. Boreman grew up in Wheeling, and, at the time of her marriage, lived in a home on the southwest corner of 5th and

Centre Streets (now Eoff and 15th) in a home originally owned by her father, Dr. James Tanner, a prominent physician, who, at the time of his death in 1858, was Wheeling's mayor. The home was only a block east of the Custom House, where the Second Wheeling Convention met, and immediately across the street from Linsly Institute, the first capitol of the new state. Did the proximity of these places allow the couple to meet?

Mrs. Boreman, the widow of John Oldham Bullock, an early casualty of the Civil War, had two sons: Talbot (b. 1855) and John (b. 1852). Two daughters were born to Arthur and Lauranne: Maud, who lived from 1866 to 1946 and Lauranne, who was born in 1867 and died in 1959. The Boreman blended family remained in Wheeling until 1869, when the governor resigned to become a United States Senator. When Boreman's term as Senator ended, the family returned to Parkersburg. The Wheeling property, however, remained in control of Mrs. Boreman.

Shortly after their marriage, a friend of the governor presented the couple with a "proper" bedroom set. It was a massive suite of carved walnut and mahogany, made in England. It took seven months for the furniture to cross the Atlantic and come down the Ohio on a steamboat. The set remained with the family until 1959.

When the former governor and senator returned to Parkersburg in 1875, he entered into a law partnership with his two stepsons. They maintained a practice in Court Square until Boreman became a circuit court judge in 1889. The practice took time to earn enough money to support the family. In 1879, the former governor was forced to demand rents that were in arrears from his wife's Wheeling property, but by the mid-1880s, he was financially secure enough to stand for election to the Circuit Court of the Fifth Judicial District, a post he won by a margin of 123 votes of the 9485 cast ballots. He remained in this post until his death in 1896.

The Boremans enjoyed a loving marriage of 32 years, and both made important contributions to the state's early history. He guided the state through the last years of the Civil War, and she established the role of First Lady for future governors' wives.

Wars often result in tragedy and heartache, as Lauranne Tanner Bullock and her sons experienced. But that same conflict brought Arthur and Lauranne together, and their marriage made possible the legal careers of her sons and successful marriages of their daughters. When Lauranne died in 1908, she was buried beside her second husband in a Parkersburg cemetery.

Wood County lawyer and judge Arthur I. Boreman presided over the Second Wheeling Convention in 1861 and was elected as the state's first governor in 1863, a position that he held until 1869. While governor, he encouraged legislation prohibiting former Confederates from voting or holding public office. He served as a U.S. Senator from 1869 until 1875, after which he returned to Parkersburg to practice law. *(Library of Congress)*

January 1865
By David Javersak

Long before Union and Confederate soldiers opposed each other on any Civil War battlefield, there was a war for the hearts and minds of American citizens. When the Virginia secessionist vote occurred on May 23, 1861, all voting districts in the Northern Panhandle of Virginia, save one in Bethany, showed overwhelming support for the Union. The villagers of West Liberty, once the seat of Ohio County government and home to a private academy, stood strong in their opposition to secession.

After President Lincoln called for suppression of the rebellion, West Liberty Academy students and faculty, local farm lads, artisans and small businessmen came together in Company D of the 12th West Virginia Infantry. This writer recently discovered a radio broadcast transcript from 1938 in which President Paul N. Elbin of West Liberty State Teachers College interviewed Maude Curtis, a lifelong resident of West Liberty and youngest daughter of Company D's commanding officer. Miss Maude asserted, "a very large percentage of the students in the [West Liberty Academy] ... enlisted to fight on the side of freedom."

David B. Rogers, West Liberty Normal Class of 1911 and once a member of its faculty, wrote this in the 1929 *West Virginia Review*. "Seventy-five of the [seventy-six students] heard Lincoln's call and rallied to the colors. A deformed body explains the discrepancy."

Given his place of birth and the date of his entry into the world, William Baker Curtis seemed predestined for military glory. He was born on the anniversary of Paul Revere's ride (April 18, 1821) at Sharpsburg, Maryland, on a farm where the Battle of Antietam was fought on September 17, 1862. He attended the Academy, and after leaving school he apprenticed as a cabinet maker in Wheeling. In 1844, he and Hannah Montgomery were married by the Academy's first principal, Nathan Shotwell, and their union produced twelve children. Very civic-minded, Curtis acted as a trustee for the Academy and held the office of Justice of the Peace.

In April 1861, he attended the First Wheeling Convention as

an Ohio County delegate, and in August, he raised the unit that became Company D and took them to Camp Carlile on Wheeling Island, where they mustered into military service. Before the unit left Wheeling for their first deployment, "the wives of the married men of the regiment, fathers, mothers, brothers, and lovers all assembled on Wheeling Island ... bringing with them provisions for a good repast." The boys set off with full bellies and "prayers ... for those brave boys who offered their services and their lives if need be for the restoration of one of the greatest Commonwealths on God's green earth."

An Academy professor, William A Smiley, joined Company D; later he rose to the rank of captain and then to paymaster. Among the many students was Josiah Montgomery Curtis, eldest son of the Curtis brood. Josiah enlisted as a private when he was still 17 years old. He served as an aide to his father thru more than a dozen campaigns, and, by war's end, he had risen to the rank of Second Lieutenant. There were three other Curtis boys: two who were too young to serve and one, Eugene, who was captured by Mosby's Raiders and sent to a prison camp near Richmond.

The 12th consisted largely of young men from Ohio County and nearby environs. They saw action at Winchester, New Market, Cedar Creek, and Opequon among other battles, and then came the assault on Fort Gregg at Petersburg on April 2, 1865. In that desperate attack, 715 officers and men were killed or wounded. For their roles on that bloody day, both Curtis men received high honors: the senior Curtis, who had previously risen to Colonel, got a promotion to General, and Josiah earned a Bronze Star and later the greatest of all American military awards – The Congressional Medal of Honor.

During the fierce fighting on that April day, two color bearers of the 12th were cut down by Confederate bullets, whereupon Josiah seized the flag. Brandishing his saber and sporting the colors, he cheered his comrades onward as bullets ripped at his jacket and a cannon shot passed between him and his flagstaff. Another Company D flag bearer, Pvt. Joseph McCauslin, also of West Liberty, earned a Medal of Honor, as did flagbearers Charles Reeder of Company G and Corporal Andrew Apple. Two years earlier, at Winchester, 2nd Lt. James R. Durham led an assault for which he received a Medal of Honor in 1890. These five members of the 12th were among the 37 West Virginians to receive their nation's highest military honor in that terrible conflict.

The West Virginia 12th mustered out on June 16, 1865, at Burksville, Virginia. The regiment had lost 190 men: 3 officers and 56 men killed in battle and 131 who died of various diseases. Long after the war's end, the survivors continued to experience war-related ailments. According to Gibson Cranmer's 1902 *History of Wheeling and Ohio County*, General Curtis "died at West Liberty, August 25, 1891 from a disease contracted while in the army." A special census of the 12th's veterans in 1890 revealed that many of these men suffered from aliments like heart disease, rheumatism, lung diseases, stomach problems, and the hardships from having lost an arm or a leg. Josiah Curtis studied medicine after his discharge and practiced in Marshall and Ohio Counties; he died from "supposed heart disease" in June 1875; he was only 30 years old.

For decades after the war's conclusion, Company D held annual reunions, often at the home of Capt. David M. Blayney of West Alexander. The final reunion of which there is a record took place in August 1917, at the United Presbyterian Church at Roney's Point, when only 12 attended.

West Liberty soldiers saw lots of action during their four years in the ranks, and they were lucky enough to be at Appomattox on April 8, 1865, when General Robert E. Lee surrendered to General Ulysses S. Grant. Their town was tiny in the 1860s – fewer than 230 folks in the 1850 census – but those West Liberty boys played a gigantic role in America's Civil War.

The Civil War resulted in lean years for West Liberty Academy, as the majority of its male students enlisted in the military, many as members of the 12th [West] Virginia Regiment under William Baker Curtis. This is the earliest known photograph of the Academy. Low enrollment led to the academy being sold to the new state of West Virginia in 1867. *(West Liberty University Archives)*

February 1865
By Joseph Laker

During February 1865 it became clear to most war-weary Americans that Confederate defeat was all but certain. On the military fronts the North dominated everywhere. Ulysses S. Grant continued to press Robert E. Lee near Richmond; William T. Sherman's soldiers ransacked South Carolina without significant opposition; Admiral David Dixon Porter seized Wilmington, North Carolina, the Confederates' last important port; Phillip Sheridan moved his troops down the Shenandoah Valley to support Grant, while George H. Thomas dominated the West. In Richmond desperate Confederate congressmen reluctantly approved of enlisting black slaves into the Confederate army, but the measure passed too late to have an impact on the war.

Although the Confederacy was collapsing, Union forces could still feel their sting as did General Benjamin Kelley, Wheeling's most important war hero. In the early morning hours of February 19th Jesse McNeill led a band of 61 Confederate guerillas on a daring, well-planned mission into Kelley's well fortified headquarters city of Cumberland, Maryland. In just 30 minutes McNeill's men kidnapped General Kelley, his commanding officer General George Crook, and Kelley's chief military aide Thayer Melvin. Although hotly pursued, the band escaped with their captives to Richmond, Virginia, and the two Generals spent a month in Libby Prison before being exchanged. Following his release Crook again took command of Union troops in the final assault on Richmond and later achieved fame in wars with the Indians in the West, but Kelley was not given another command and resigned from the army shortly after the end of the war.

Politically, Lincoln's position was strengthened when the Electoral College formally voted the President into office for a second term. Lincoln received 212 electoral votes to just 21 for his Democratic challenger, General George McClellan. In the previous month of January both the United States Senate and House of Representatives voted in favor of the 13th amendment to the

Constitution. The amendment would eliminate slavery if ratified by twenty-seven of the thirty-six states. Illinois was the first to ratify on February 1st. West Virginia was the sixth when voting on February 3rd, but it was not until December 11, 1865, that the 27th vote was achieved. Wheeling's newspapers reflected a divided people on the question. The *Intelligencer* exulted when West Virginia ratified the amendment, but the *Daily Register* condemned the vote as unnecessary and unconstitutional.

An attempt at peace talks occurred on February 3rd when a Confederate delegation led by Alexander Stephens, the Confederacy's Vice-President, and two other Southern leaders met for four hours with President Lincoln and Secretary of State William Seward aboard a U. S. warship at Hampton Roads, Virginia. The talks were amiable, but failed almost at once when Lincoln demanded that the Confederates first recognize the national authority of the United States government. Lincoln also said there would be no receding on the slavery issue as the 13th amendment was in the process of being ratified and that all forces hostile to the Union must be disbanded.

On February 8, 1865, Mayor Andrew J. Sweeney gave a "State of the City" report to the two Wheeling council chambers. He called on the councilors to support eight reform proposals. The speech provides interesting insights on how the city of almost 18,000 operated near the end of the war. First, he asked the councils to authorize city authorities to control and pay for all celebrations to honor and respect soldiers rather than allow private groups, which he claimed had excluded too many people in the past and had been expressions of political partisanship.

The mayor also called for a huge expansion of Wheeling's police force, which then consisted of a City-Sergeant and seven men, one for each ward, under his command. Sweeney claimed there had been an increase in crime, drunkenness, and rowdiness, and the people were demanding protection. He called for a force of thirty-one men who would be organized into three shifts. The mayor called for the building of a city prison that would be separate from the County Jail. He also demanded that Council authorize the replacement of many of the city's water pipes, which were too old and small to provide water to the new steam fire trucks. He argued that the city needed to produce a new book of city ordinances as the current one was ten years old and much legislation had been changed since its issuance. Sweeney argued that the city should determine the hours of operation at the city markets to enable farmers to come and sell their wares and return home the same day. He also claimed that the city should open the old City Hall as a city market. Finally, he called for the council to replace its system of Aldermen with a well-paid, full-time judge to end excessive and abusive litigation.

The bitterness and divisions among war-weary West Virginians was frequently seen in proposed bills in both houses of the legislature. The *Intelligencer* reported on a proposal in the House of Delegates that would deny voting rights to all who had borne arms against the state, opposed the Reorganized Government of Virginia, borne arms against the United States, or gave aid and comfort to the enemy. Fortunately, wiser heads prevailed, and the bill died.

Near the end of the month, the Wheeling newspapers provided extensive coverage of the trial to impeach Judge John Kennedy of the West Virginia Circuit Court. The trial illustrated the deep divisions caused by the war in the city and state. Strong Unionists in the West Virginia legislatures accused Kennedy of pro-Confederate sympathies, questioning the legitimacy of West Virginia's government, not holding court regularly, and appointing disloyal persons to public office. The House voted to remove Kennedy 29 to 19, while the Senate total was 15 to 5. The *Intelligencer* favored Kennedy's impeachment, but the Wheeling *Daily Register* decried the result and claimed that a good and decent man was being unjustly attacked for partisan reasons.

Andrew J. Sweeney served a total of nine terms as Mayor of Wheeling. Well after the Civil War, he is credited with bringing electricity to the city. *(Wheeling Hall of Fame)*

By Kate Quinn

March of 1865 was a month of dread and tension. With the river at 30 feet and rising, the city waited to see just how bad things would get. The island was already under water, and one observer stated that it looked "like a gem in the ocean." With Lincoln's inaugural ball on the horizon, women despaired over the cost of silks and brocades, while cotton was in short supply. Many women anxiously awaited a return of relatives from Southern prisons as there had been no exchange in quite a while. A sense of tension in the air was prevalent everywhere, especially in the army camps as everyone waited to see how long Robert E. Lee could last against the Union forces.

Meanwhile, Major General George Crook and General Benjamin F. Kelley were captured in Cumberland and sent to Richmond. They were lucky in not being sent to Andersonville, the worst of the Confederate prisons, where several Wheeling men languished. Andersonville Prison was built in February 1864 by slave labor and covered 16 acres in southwestern Georgia. Designed to hold 10,000 prisoners, it actually contained nearly 30,000. It was enlarged to about 30 acres later, but there was no shelter provided for the men, and they lived in the open space. A fence was erected 19 feet inside the outer walls and was nicknamed "the deadline" since prisoners who even touched the fence or reached over it were shot. Stockade Creek ran through the prison and was the only source of water for both drinking and bathing. It soon became polluted, resulting in thousands of cases of dysentery. In addition to illness from disease and exposure, many men died from malnutrition and starvation.

Among the Confederate soldiers at the prison was a baker from Wheeling named James Duncan who had joined the Confederacy after moving to Louisiana. He was appointed to be the baker for Andersonville prison in a facility located outside the stockade. He searched out and found many Union prisoners from Wheeling and gave them work in the bakery plus extra rations, saving many lives. After the war Duncan was accused of murdering a prisoner, feeding rations to his hogs, and stealing packages from home intended for the prisoners. His trial took place in Savannah in 1866, and five former prisoners from Wheeling went to testify on his behalf. The identity of the murdered man was never found, yet Duncan was found guilty of most of the charges and sentenced to fifteen years hard labor at Fort Pulaski. Obviously, the judge was prejudiced against a Northerner who had aided and abetted the prisoners from his hometown.

Sixteen people including Daniel Lamb, one of Wheeling's most prominent men, signed a petition to President Andrew Johnson asking for the release of Duncan to no avail. Duncan himself wrote to the President stating that his family (wife, mother-in-law, and four children) was suffering extreme hardship without his support. Again, his pleas went unanswered. On July 11, 1867, Duncan escaped the prison with the help of former prisoners that he had befriended and moved to Philadelphia.

Justice was served also, when the Commandant of Andersonville, Captain Henry Wirz was convicted and executed for war crimes in August of 1865. Over 100 prisoners were called to testify against him.

In the month of April of 1865, just after the assassination of President Lincoln, America's greatest maritime disaster took place when the over-crowded steamboat *Sultana* exploded on the Mississippi. The boat was carrying mostly prisoners from Andersonville, and 75% of the 2300 ex-prisoners on board died as a result of the explosion. Since most of the soldiers were from the Midwest and the major newspapers were in the East, the story was buried, and few are aware of it today.

The overloaded *Sultana* carried several Wheeling soldiers who had survived imprisonment at the infamous Confederate prison at Andersonville, Georgia. A few survived after the April 27 explosion of the riverboat and returned to Wheeling. News of the death of John Wilkes Booth the day before overshadowed this disaster. *(Library of Congress)*

April 1865
By John Bowman

By April 1865, the war was over, the country was torn, and there was jubilation for the North, despair for the South, and a Nation in mourning for the loss of President Lincoln.

April 1st saw the defeat of General Robert E. Lee's forces at the Battle of Five Forks, culminating with the "Breakthrough" and Ulysses S. Grant's capture of Petersburg and twelve thousand Rebel soldiers April 2nd. That morning, Lee sent word to Confederate President Jefferson Davis that he and the government should immediately evacuate Richmond, and Lee with his remaining forces would evacuate Petersburg that evening.

On April 3rd, Union forces occupied Richmond, and the next day President Lincoln left Grant's Field Headquarters at City Point where he had met with Generals Grant and William T. Sherman and, aboard the *River Queen*, steamed up the James River to Richmond. President Lincoln with a small group of soldiers, his son Tad, and an entourage of former slaves, visited the abandoned Confederate White House and State House and made a further visit to Libby Prison.

President Lincoln's meeting with Generals Grant and Sherman, scribed by Admiral David Dixon Porter, instructed each that if "Lee and Johnston surrendered, he considered the war ended." Lincoln's quote, "Let them surrender and go home... let them have their horses to plow with and, if you like, their guns to shoot crows with... Give them the most liberal and honorable of terms." With this in mind, General Sherman returned to Goldsboro, North Carolina.

On April 6th, General Lee's army suffered a devastating loss at the Battle of Sayler's (Sailor's) Creek, where it became clear to Lee that the end was near and that his Army of Northern Virginia was disintegrating. Union Forces had captured one third of Lee's remaining army, 7,700 men including six of his Generals. On April 7th, Lee with the remaining 27,800 men in his army, headed west where food supplies awaited him at Appomattox Station. On April 8th, Lee found his army trapped and wrote to Grant asking for a peace deal. Grant replied with a letter to Lee setting out Lincoln's terms and that Grant would parole Lee's officers and men. On April 9th, Lee responded to Grant, "I have received your letter of this date containing the terms of surrender as proposed by you and they are accepted."

On the afternoon of April 9 at the Wilmer McLean House near the small village of Appomattox Court House, Lee and Grant met. Lee, neatly dressed in a spotless gray uniform rode in on a borrowed gray horse, accompanied by his Aide-de Camp, Colonel Charles Marshall, and Johns, his orderly. The two Generals made small talk about their service in Mexico but quickly moved on with the terms of surrender, which Grant wrote out. Lee wrote his formal acceptance, and at four p.m. Lee signed the paper, rose, and made his exit. Mounting his horse, Lee raised his hat respectfully to Grant and rode off to break the news to his Army. Grant announced the surrender to his joyous men, telling them, "The war is over; the Rebels are our countrymen again."

On April 14, the War Department sent this dispatch: "This evening about half past nine o'clock, at Ford's Theatre, the President, while sitting in his private box with Mrs. Lincoln, Mrs. Harris and Major Rathbourn, was shot by an assassin, who suddenly entered the box, approached behind the President and shot him. The pistol ball entered the back of the President's head, penetrating nearly through the head. The President has been insensible ever since it was inflicted and is now dying. Having fired the shot, the assassin then leaped upon the stage brandishing a large knife, and made his escape in the rear of the Theatre." A hat belonging to John Wilkes Booth was found in the President's private box and identified by several persons. The spur that he dropped by accident after he jumped to the stage, was also identified as one of those which Booth had obtained from the stable where he hired his horse.

The official announcement of the "Death of President Lincoln" Washington, April 15, stated, "Abraham Lincoln died this morning at twenty-two minutes after seven o'clock," signed E. M. Stanton,

Secretary of War. At eleven a.m., Chief Justice Salmon P. Chase swore Andrew Johnson into office as President of the United States. President Johnson remarked, "The duties are mine."

Stanton announced, "The President's body was removed from the private residence of Mrs. Peterson, opposite Ford's Theatre to the Executive mansion this morning at nine-thirty. An autopsy was held this p.m., over the body of President Lincoln by Surgeon General Barnes and Dr. Stone and the remains were embalmed. A few locks of hair were removed from the President's head for the family, previous to the remains being placed in the coffin. The coffin is of mahogany and is covered with black cloth and lined with lead, the latter being covered with white satin." A silver plate upon the coffin, over the breast bears the following inscription: 'Abraham Lincoln, Sixteenth President of the United States, born July 12th, 1809, died April 15th, 1865.'" President Lincoln's funeral would be held April 19th.

The *Evening Star* of April 27 reported that a detachment of the 16th New York cavalry killed the assassin Booth, having been traced to a barn near Port Royal. The barn was set afire, and Booth, making a bolt, was shot in the neck by Sergeant Boston Corbett and died. Booth, before breathing his last, replied, "Tell my mother that I died for my country." The body of Booth was taken to the Navy Yard.

On April 26th, at the farm home of James Bennett, Confederate General Joseph E. Johnston surrendered 89,270 Confederate soldiers to Union General William T. Sherman, the largest group, on either side, to surrender during the Civil War.

On April 27th, the steamer *Sultana* with 1,886 Federal troops, ex-prisoners of war aboard, exploded her boilers killing most of those on board.

Wheeling, where the "Child of the Rebellion" was born, sent soldiers to both sides during the war, which had cost the nation the lives of 360,000 Union and 260,000 Confederate soldiers.

This building, the former Linsly Military Institute, served as the first capitol of West Virginia from June 20, 1863, to April 1, 1870. It was also the site of the inauguration of West Virginia's first governor, Arthur I. Boreman. The Thirteenth amendment to the U.S. Constitution, enacted in 1865 (calling for the abolishment of slavery), the Fourteenth amendment, enacted in 1868, (prohibiting states from depriving any person of life, liberty or property without "due process"), and the Fifteenth amendment, enacted in 1870, (prohibiting the abridgement of the right to vote on the basis of race, color, or previous condition of servitude) were all ratified in this building. *(Ohio County Public Library Archives)*